Wanted:
Gentleman Bank Robber

The True Story of Leslie Ibsen Rogge, One
of the FBI's Most Elusive Criminals

Dane Batty

Hillsboro, Oregon

Wanted: Gentleman Bank Robber
The True Story of Leslie Ibsen Rogge, One of the FBI's Most Elusive Criminals

880 NE 25th Avenue
Suite 2-102
Hillsboro, Oregon 97124
www.lesrogge.com;
info@lesrogge.com

Cover by Lesley Rogge
Interior design by Robin Simonds, Beagle Bay, Inc.

ISBN 978-0-615-2684-5-3
LCCN 2009936173

First Edition

Printed in the USA
15 14 13 12 11 10   1 2 3 4 5 6 7 8 9 10

Dedication

Dane Batty

This book is dedicated to my mother, whose idea it was to create a memoir of my uncle's stories and share them with the world. There is nobody that cares more than Mum, an angel from above, and whose constant support and needed help was inspiration enough.

Introduction

This is the true story of Leslie Ibsen Rogge, who robbed nearly thirty banks over the span of twenty years. Les escaped from custody three times, with one jail escape that made him so famous it landed him at number seven on the FBI's Top Ten Most Wanted List. He eluded the FBI and U.S. Marshall's office for ten years before surrendering and becoming the first ever Top Ten FBI-wanted fugitive in history to surrender due to the World Wide Web.

While on the run, Les traveled all over the U.S., from Alaska to New Mexico, through the Midwest and East Coast, and down to Key West. He also managed to fit in tours of the Caribbean, Mexico and finally, Guatemala.

Les's bank robbery skills didn't start out as sophisticated as they ended. He developed them as he went along, rejecting the "how to" information he picked up in prison, and finally coming up with an "M.O." that earned him the nickname The Gentleman Bandit. Les mostly worked alone and used a professional appearance, often wearing a nice suit and carrying a briefcase to allay his prey's suspicions. He gave the impression he was a millionaire with money to transfer from another bank. By making appointments with bank managers and timing his robberies to coincide with lunch hours or just prior to closing time, Les was able to succeed in every bank he robbed. His calm and polite manner avoided panic and the need for gunplay.

Les used smarts, tactics, persuasion and moments of brilliance to rob banks. His best skill was being able to scope out the banks that had the right "robbing attributes" that he was looking for. Early on, he discovered that male bank employees would try to be heroic, so he looked for all-female staffs. He would thoroughly calculate and plan very creative getaways using stolen and planted vehicles. Many times he used boats, and once, even a stolen plane. He used the best electronics of the day, such as police scanners and police radios. Often he carried electronic components with prominently blinking LEDs to know if the bank staff had tripped the alarms—or at least he tricked them into thinking his devices detected alarms. All of his acquired skills were self-taught using his own ingenuity, patience and practice. He even taught himself how to fly an airplane, and became a skilled sailor.

I calculate that Les stole over $2 million dollars over his twenty year bank robbing career. He pulled off incredible bank robberies where he came away with huge sums of money, and others that failed completely. Both kinds of "jobs" are here in this story, and some are incredibly funny. He didn't take himself very seriously, and he never let ego get in his way. Les is not a violent man; in fact he was fairly scared of danger, so he usually left when the situation turned dangerous.

After his amazing jail escape, Les eluded authorities for over ten years before his surrender. There were U.S. Marshals and FBI agents dedicated to his capture that followed him wherever he went, even outside American borders. They spread untruths to entire communities. Using the TV show "America's Most Wanted," they devoted many episodes to cast the widest dragnet possible in hopes of making a capture. The FBI raided the homes of relatives and friends in towns wherever he went. Many people were interrogated simply because they had talked to Les, and amazingly most of them forgave Les for the treatment they got by the authorities simply because he was such a good friend. Most of these people, once they knew what Les did for a living, didn't turn him in or even testify against him, and their lives were worse afterward for it.

My Involvement

Les is my uncle—he is my mother's brother. After he was imprisoned in 1996, he would send short stories about his life of crime to my mother (Mum) from time to time, and she would let me read and enjoy them. Those tales were funny, adventurous, exciting. . . and best of all, true. Mum cherished the letters and her relationship with Les and never failed to love him with all of her heart.

When I would share these letters with my friends, everyone was astounded. I knew that there was a book there from the beginning.

I wanted to document those letters, put them in writing and make them available for future genera- tions. Mum kept the hand- and some- times typewritten- letters in a plastic bin. I just knew that over the years they were going to get ru- ined and lost to the world. So, in 2000, I gathered the stories and put them in the

Les and author/nephew Dane. 1973

computer. I ended up with an incomplete mishmash that was completely without any timeline. I sent these stories to Les in hopes that he would arrange the order for me, and instead he started over and helped me write his story. The new story was chronologically correct, but it lacked the details of the individual tales, so I used the original, detailed stories to supplement the larger, less developed and newer version.

With the help of interviews with people Les was close with, and researching the robberies through court documents, testimonials, newspaper articles and television shows, the result is a detailed, chronologically correct life story that focuses on the highlights of Les's life of crime and adventures. The text you'll find in italics are my comments or narrative fill-ins.

I tried to contact the authorities for information for this book, but the U.S. Marshal's agency didn't have any record of the people who visited the families during Les's reign whose business cards I had obtained. After the escape, every family member got visited by the FBI on the anniversary of Les's escape every year, and you could count on it. Les's crimes, at the time this book was written, were all over twenty years old. The agents have a mandatory retirement of twenty or so years. So even if Les were their first case, they still would have been retired by the time I came looking for them. The Marshall's human resource agency wouldn't forward a message or attempt to find people for me for obvious reasons.

The local FBI was uncooperative in helping me research information. The most cooperative people were the clerks or the stenographers that sold me transcripts from Les's court cases they had kept in their archives. Although they didn't turn out to be good sources of information for the book, they were interesting. I'm sure it would help to be a lawyer when reviewing these, but I do owe a big thank you to the lovely ladies all over the country who helped me graciously, (Les had a bunch of trials) and charged me little, to gather the information that I needed.

This started out as a project of documenting the individual stories for my Mum but has turned out to be one of the most gratifying goals I have ever accomplished. With having a full-time job, a full-time family with children, and keeping my life in a normal mode, I am very happy that I have completed this bigger-than-life goal. I hope you enjoy the story as much as I have.

Please note I have changed some names to protect the innocent and hide the guilty.

The Double

My partner, Bo, and I were pretty successful. So much so that we bought a condo in the Houston area, furnished it and had a car in the garage for an emergency getaway. We sat around night after night getting stoned and trying to come up with original ideas to make money. Since Bo was broke, we decided that we would do two banks, one after the other, and use the distraction of the first to reduce the police presence at the second. We also wanted a natural barrier between the banks, some type of separation that would slow down the response from the first bank to the second. The simplest would be mountains or a river, something natural. It was in the fall, so we wanted to stay in the South and didn't want to go more than a day and a night away. We planned on taking my motor home and leaving my wife, Linda, and the car. We would be gone a week, max. Linda had no idea.

After scattering maps all over the floor, we came up with two possibilities. The first was East and West Memphis with the Mississippi River in between the two. The second was Baton Rouge with the same barrier. We ruled Memphis number two and turned our attention to Baton Rouge. The big city was on the east of the river, and little Baton Rouge on the west side was on the way home back to Houston. Things were coming together, and we took off going east on I-10.

The Double

We found a trailer court on Baton Rouge's east side that was real low-key. Very easily, we acquired all the frequencies for the scanner. In town, we found very detailed maps of the entire community and fire department maps showing the grids that sometimes made a big difference as to how the police react to major crimes.

It was time to go to work and find every bank in the area and put them on our maps including cop shops, sub-stations, highway patrol and county sheriff stations. The biggest part of the city, about 400 thousand people, was separated by the river from the 20 thousand on the west, so it seemed logical that we would hit one on the east, come west and hit number two, then leave on the freeway west. Baton Rouge-proper was a big challenge. It is a southern town, with mostly blacks, with a medium to high crime rate—that meant a lot of police. Our frequency director books showed how many cop cars and radios, how many hand-helds (street cops) and how many repeaters, and the same research went into the highway trooper and parish cops. Most of the time, we listened to the scanners main net for crimes and how they were handled. Although by law all the radio transmitting in the U.S. must have a license from the FCC, the cops would use a few other frequencies for their top crimes that they for sure didn't want people to listen to. If a crime happened, the dispatcher might say, "All detectives to Tac Number One." People don't know about the frequency, so they didn't get to listen. When this happened, I would turn my scanner to scan and try to find the frequency they were on. After a few nights and a weekend, I could begin to figure out their methods of operation, including where their "eyes in the skies" were and their hours as well. It was information that could make or break a good robbery.

During the next few days, we decided on a bank. We checked, and rechecked, and checked again the car transfer point and getaway. We used right turns only, because a left turn could turn into two-to-three minutes of waiting for traffic. We also developed a place where two people could get out of one car and into another without any witnesses. It would have looked very suspicious if we were seen. In practice, sometimes we would just pull up and one person would get out and follow the other for a couple blocks, then the driver would stop and get out. On all our jobs, it was something we worked out. On this job, we had to figure out if we were going to keep the first car or take time to switch before crossing the bridge to the second bank.

We went through the want ads to find a reliable junker for the first car, and maybe a second. We couldn't make up our minds if we needed one or two cars, so we decided to go with two to be safe: a white Chevy and a black Volvo. Both cars looked liked shit, but they fit our criteria of quick-starting, had OK tires and up-to-date tags and inspection stickers.

Finally, we decided on our first bank, which was staffed by women. It was about two-and-a-half miles from the big bridge. It was sort of on the edge of a residential area. There was an easy exit to the main street and an adjacent residential street where we could change cars or follow the street all the way back to the bridge on-ramp by staying off the main avenue. For some reason, cops always want to go to the bank *after* it's been robbed. They know you won't be there, but they still go. It was important that these on-the-scene law-types were misled from the start. We always made it a point to give a witness a good look at the getaway car, since that information would be relayed to the cops—say a white Chevy with tags number so-and-so—but that car would never be on the road for more than a couple minutes and never on a main street. If we did it right, the car would be left somewhere where it wouldn't be found for a while and that would give us plenty of safe time to leave the area.

The second bank was quite small, with three women and one drive-up window. We liked drive-up windows, since they would have more money on certain days like the first and the fifteenth for local paydays. That bank had a great getaway. Three blocks after leaving, we would head for the back roads that could get us to a west-bound freeway rest area—a slick getaway. It all looked good, except we didn't want to leave the Volvo at the rest area. If it was found too fast, it would show another car transfer going west. We didn't want to drive the Volvo down the freeway behind the motor home, or to some-place else to ditch it. We decided to leave the car at a 7-Eleven about eight blocks from the trailer park, which was far enough to distance the Volvo from the park. We would walk to the mo-tor home with backpacks.

Next, we had to decide when we wanted to do the job. The first bank would be the big money bank, since it was located right at the end of a small mall, so it would have the night depos-its. That meant the best time was Monday morning before the armored truck did its pick-up. Bank Two was just a potluck; we really didn't know what to expect. It was small enough that we could take our time and clean out the vault, and we thought we might just get lucky and find some gold coins or something valu-able. So we decided that Monday at approximately 9:45 a.m. was our target. The bank opened at nine, so the rush would prob-ably be over. We had to get there before the armored car pick-up came. If we timed it right, the money would be in the bags just waiting for us, and we would use the remainder of the time to pick up the rest in the vault.

The rest of the week, we worked to finish all the details. We wanted traveler's checks—American Express was the best. We didn't want to try to get those at Bank One because it would take too much time and more bags. We planned on taking some blank cashier's checks if they were easy, but we mainly planned on going for all the twenties, fifties and hundreds. If there were customers in the lobby we planned on just skipping the tellers,

at us or anything threatening. We left a trail straight to the main drag, then two rights back behind the mall to our residential road to the bridge.

Bo tapped his ear piece as I played with the scanner bands. "We got smoke," he said. "The smoke bomb went off on schedule."

We picked up the Volvo and threw in my two bags, attaché case and Bo's two bags. Two minutes later, we were on the bridge. After two exits, we turned off and pulled into a furniture store parking lot and put the bags in the trunk and committed ourselves to Bank Two, which was six blocks away. All was quiet on the scanner on that side of the river. Not much was on the east side news—except a bank robbery and smoke at the mall! They said two men in suits, armed, left in a white sedan—but they didn't have the tags. That was great.

We thought we would wait and more action would cover us, but after fifteen minutes Bo said, "Let's do it!" Then my adrenaline really went up.

We pulled into the bank lot, and there was only one car, plus the cashiers' cars on the side. I parked almost in front, out of the line-of-sight, but as close to the door as possible. I got out with the attaché case, went in and walked straight over to the counter where I waited. There was only one customer at a teller, and I had to wait—funny! No wonder people hate banks. I waited until someone looked up and saw me, but the lady who asked if she could help me wasn't the manager.

I ran the line about being a new customer, but she said she could handle it. So I said, "I'm looking for a personal-type bank and I'd like to sit down with a manager."

What could she say but, "One moment."

She went over to the manager's desk. Instead of motioning me over to her desk, the manager got up and came over to the counter.

The Double

This is not going right. I stood firm and asked, "Can we sit down and go over my requirements for a new bank?"

"OK, sure, come in," she said.

At the end of the counter was a little swing door with a clever little finger lock combination to open from the inside, but she opened it and signaled me past. I couldn't see how she opened it, but I decided to worry about that later. We sat down and she introduced herself. I just pulled out the same robbery letter that I had just used across the river and handed it to her.

She read it and asked, "Are you serious?"

"Yes, ma'am. Are you going to cooperate or am I going to have to shoot you?" I replied.

"Oh, of course I'll cooperate."

"Please call your vault clerk over."

"We don't have a vault clerk. I have the responsibility for that," she said.

I told her, "Hold on a second." I made her wait until Bo came in. I turned on the scanner and told her it was monitoring her alarm system. Bo's timing was perfect, so the manager and I got up. At that time there was nobody in the place but us.

The manager told the other girls, "These men are robbing us. Please cooperate with them."

Bo further told the cashiers what to do and what would happen if he found a money pack of bait or a dye pack in the money they gave him.

The manager and I went to the vault. She opened the large stainless steel door of the safe. I opened my case and handed her a nylon bag. She filled it, and I asked her, "Is this all?"

She said, "The rest is at the teller's cages." Which meant that Bo had already gotten that cash.

"OK, I said, let's go." As we passed her desk, I picked up the scanner. It was silent.

17

I hopped over the gate and I was out! I said, "Thank you for your cooperation and don't come outside!" And we ran out.

We'd left the key in the trunk lock to save time. Bo threw his bag in the trunk. I kept my bag and case with me, hopped in the driver's seat and started out. The car was moving when Bo hopped in.

Our exit was made to look like we were heading for the freeway, but of course we turned the other way in two blocks and headed down our getaway to the back of the trailer park. We always carried a box of plastic garbage bags in case we got lucky, and our bags were not adequate. It was the kind of job we hoped for—the mother lode! In fact, we had too many bags to carry in one trip!

We parked in our chosen spot, and it was totally cool. There wasn't anybody around in any direction. I kept a box knife in my case, and I sure was happy because the bank bags had a lock on them. We needed to dump them into a plastic garbage bag to be able to make just one trip. There wasn't all that much money, but it was just too many bags to carry. And it would look mighty weird to be seen carrying four bank bags, two smaller bags and my case. So we cut the bags and dumped them all into two plastic garbage bags, and it made a much better load. We had worn ladies nylon gloves, like panty hose, that came in all shades. I don't know what they were for, perhaps glove liners, but they were great. They left no prints in the cars.

I left the keys in the Volvo and hefted a bag over my shoulder that also had my suit coat and shoulder holster in it.

Before we left the car, we took a moment to think back about if we forgot anything. Bo asked, "Do we have everything?"

Everything seemed fine. "OK, let's go!" I said. With my tieless white shirt and sleeves rolled up I didn't look too bad. It seemed like a long walk to the back of the trailer park, but it really wasn't. It was just the adrenaline pumping. We were on the home stretch! If a cop drove by, he would have surely given us a look, but none did. Ten minutes later, we entered the back of the park and crossed to the motor home. As far as we could tell, nobody noticed.

It was weird, but right then I started shaking so bad I had trouble with the key. Once inside, we high-fived, mixed a strong shot and downed a beer. Bo turned on the scanner, and they were just then talking about us. They had a great description of the Volvo and the tag numbers. I hoped some high school kid would steal the car before it was found. Bo wanted to stay, count the money and get high, but I vetoed that.

I told him, "You can count the money on the freeway. We are out of here!"

I unhooked the power cord, water and sewer hose and pulled around to the office to check out. We owed nothing extra. I went over to the phones and called Linda to tell her we were on the freeway, coming home. Back in the office, I bought a twelve-pack of beer and a bag of ice for our little cooler. Then we hit the road. I set the cruise control for two miles an hour over the posted speed limit and stayed in the right lane. We had 340 miles and six hours to go. I hit the stereo to hear, "On the Road Again"!

Bo had a ball counting the money and finding little surprises: a few gold coins, some two dollar bills, a big handful of cashier's checks that were blank and traveler's checks. Not a bad two weeks! It was a bit hard on the nerves, but considering we made about $40 thousand in a week each, it was worth it!

friends, he gave me the option of waiting in the lobby or in the car—but he didn't trust me with his keys. There really wasn't any reason for me to have the keys since the radio stations were boring for kids in those days. Most autos around that time had an ignition switch and a starter button. To get the button to work, you had to have the key turned on. That presented a problem that I just had to solve—because I wanted to start that car!

After studying the back of the key switch—which meant looking up behind the dash of Dad's Ford Mercury—I found the answer to my problem. I decided that all the switch did was connect the wires together when turned on—no big mystery. I could connect the wires from the back of the switch, and then the start button would work. I connected the wires together and the starter howled! Then I found the one fat wire that did this and it all became clear. After a few trials, I discovered that if the key was turned to the left, the radio would work, but the start button would not. I needed a gizmo with alligator clips to attach to the wires on the back of the key switch and one wire that

Sister Jeannie and Les Rogge. 1954

clipped to the fat wire that had to work for a moment. At home, I found that a doorbell button would work for that.

In my bedroom with the stuff that I had found in my dad's workshop, I created a gizmo with four alligator clips with a button attached. With this attached to the back of any switch, I could start a car in seconds after ducking under the dash for a moment. Success! That led to the next stage—start the car and drive!

Hotel Edmundson was on the corner of 45th and one block off of University in the U district of Seattle where I transferred buses to go home from school. In the basement of this hotel was a garage full of cars with nobody around—and all unlocked, as cars tended to be in those days. They didn't have keys in the ignition, so that was where my gizmo was field-tested. It was a very gratifying experience to be able to defeat Detroit's effort at car security, and I got to drive any car at Hotel Edmundson that I wanted.

Being a kid, I didn't think too far in advance. I should have known that a sudden abundance of abandoned Ford and Mercury cars around my neighborhood would soon bring the police knocking on our door. Someone had noticed me leaving one of the cars and walking home. That experience, of course, only showed me that there were broader horizons to explore. How about driving a nice car all night or for an entire weekend? Thus a career was born.

Somehow, after all that, I managed to talk myself into a driver's license of my own. I believe the deal was at fifteen I could drive in the daytime if I was a farm boy (which I was not). I managed to persuade my sweet old mom into signing me up for one under those conditions. I bought my first car for twenty dollars—an old Chevy Sedan with a driveshaft problem; it wouldn't drive. We lived in a nice but tiny house with no room to park a disabled car. But across the street, our neighbor had some room. I talked him into letting me park my Chevy in his yard while it was under repair. My dad said I wouldn't ever be able to fix it in a driveway—which was the only reason I was allowed to buy it in the first place. He thought I would never get it running. The enclosed front universal joint was broken, and that necessitated removing the entire drive train. That was not a driveway job! I was determined to get that thing running so I could drive it.

Taking the entire car apart was beyond me, but then I found out the library was good for something other than homework. I found a picture of my problem in a repair manual, and that wonderful book showed me all sorts of stuff that I was wondering about and stuff my dad was tired of telling me about. One Saturday, while my neighbors and my folks were partying, my Chevy and I took our first drive. My own car—it was bliss. Of course, when my folks found out that I got it running they grounded me, but it was short-lived. Insurance was a priority for Dad, so he covered his ass by adding the Chevy to his business. Soon though, the Chevy wasn't good enough, as some of my friends didn't want to be seen in it—not to mention the girls' reactions. So my next goal was a better car.

One of my Dad's salesmen quit or got fired, but his company car was parked at our house. It was obvious to me that the car needed a caretaker. It was a '55 Ford—less than a year old—a two-door, blue-on-blue, straight-stick with a radio. Even though it was a square car, it was very nice. Dad let me drive it on dates, and I talked Mom into letting me drive it more. That turned into almost every day after school. "Be home before Dad," she would tell me. At that time, Dad was doing big things, and he wasn't home much. Mom had my little sister to care for, and my brother just showed up, so I was sort of the man around the house.

I managed to acquire about forty speeding tickets in one summer during my early high school days. I was called into court to face the judge. I couldn't pay the fines, and knew I faced jail time if I didn't think of something—fast. So I just started talking to the judge. I'm not sure what happened, but I just kept talking and talking. Next thing you know, the judge said he felt sorry for me, and set me free!

I got thrown out of Roosevelt High School. The school principal was a crusty old guy who didn't put up with anything. That meant I had to go to Ballard High School, which was way across town. I was mostly driving to school at this time, and only home to beg for gas money. Then everything changed. Dad sold the car, and we moved to Edmonds, north of the city, to a nice big brick house with a bedroom for each of us, and a big driveway with a two-car garage and lots of trees. It was very nice. Mom's Dad and Mom had passed away, and she inherited her own car that was a nice Dodge. Dad started his succession of Chryslers where he got a fancy new one each year; money wasn't a problem then. I got a job at the corner gas station pumping gas, and my mom cosigned a note so I could buy my own car—a 1950 Ford Coupe.

At the gas station, I was working nights mostly on my own car. I put every new part on it that I could swipe. It was my senior year of high school when my girlfriend Lois and I decided to run away. I swiped all the credit cards I could find in my dad's desk in the basement—he had to have them all since they were a new thing. So Lois and I took off for ten weeks using dad's credit cards; we drove the Ford everywhere. We never needed cash because at gas stations I would say, "Put a case of oil on the card." Instead of giving me the oil, I'd ask for cash instead. This worked out lovely.

Of course, we had nowhere to go, and after calling home, we returned. Lois's mom wanted me thrown in jail for violating her daughter. I ended up going to juvenile court. The judge told me, "The girl's mom wants you out of the picture, so I'll give you four choices—now pick a service. It's time you grew up."

Les in Navy. 1958-9.

I picked the Navy for the boats, and away I went to boot camp in 1957.

After finishing boot camp I was assigned to radar school in San Francisco and then a destroyer out in San Diego which was real close to Mexico! After a couple of years of cruising around the South Pacific, I was transferred to Long Beach, California, and another destroyer. I was a Quartermaster and not liking the dark radar room. I wanted to be on the bridge where the action was. So that didn't work out for me very well.

I had my first set of phony I.D. and started tending bar at night. I was driving a car that I had tested—with every intention of buying—but I just kept it. Although I got caught and had to serve a few months in jail for the car theft before returning to the Navy, it wasn't until I went AWOL for the second time that I was discharged from the Navy under Less than Honorable Conditions.

My Navy days came to an end in 1961, just like my time at my four different high schools, but I had learned some good useful skills for my career ahead as well as completing my GED.

After his Navy days, Les was to spend some minor time in a jail for cashing some non-sufficient checks and a petty theft charge while he was in Long Beach, California. When he was being arraigned, he talked the judge out of being arrested on the spot and into letting him drive himself to the jail facility. He was going to serve sixty days and three years probation, but since the charges were misdemeanors they didn't come looking for him when he simply didn't report for jail.

Les got married in 1962, and he and Joan had a good relationship. She really loved Les—as did everyone. She was wild, too, so their lifestyle was very fun-loving. When Les's children Troy and Tracy were young, Les's mom would babysit until she became ill with cancer. They were close to the family and used to go out with his sister, Jeannie (Mum), and her husband Joe. Joan was close with Jeannie during the first few years—they were only eighteen months apart and enjoyed each other. As Les's adventures grew, he was too wild to be a good father, and she could not put up with the irresponsibility any longer.

In 1966, I managed a 76 Union gas station at the bottom of Queen Ann Hill in Seattle, with a large parking area. People often came to me, asking me to help them get a car for a good price, so I did that from time to time.

A customer of mine called. "I've got to have one of the new Eldorados in triple black—damn the cost!"

The '67 Cadillac Eldorados were out and extremely hot. Every big roller wanted one, but back then Cadillac allotted cars to dealers. You could never get all the cars you wanted, and with the Eldos it was worse—I think my friend the Cadillac dealer was allotted about fifteen for the year. New, they sold loaded for about $8 to 9 thousand. What the guy wanted was another order of expensive: "triple black" meant black trim, black leather and a black padded top. Well shit, we were talking about $10 thousand! That was some money in those days (my rent was about $150). So I decided to try and get one.

I called my friend Wild Bill who was living in Long Beach, California. We used to own a dragster together when I lived down there. Wild Bill was also in the car business, and I told

L to R: Les's son, Troy, and daughter, Tracy, with brother, Rob.

him I'd pay him a grand if he could find a triple black Eldo for me in his area. He told me, "For a grand, I'll send my lot boy out to steal one tonight!"

I really didn't believe him, and we had a good laugh.

Two days, later he called to tell me, "I got your Eldo. What do you want me to do with it!?"

I said, "Oh shit, really? Let me call you back."

I called the customer: "I found a triple black Eldorado, but it's going to cost $2 thousand over window sticker, in cash." There was no way I could finance a bootlegged new car.

He told me, "I've been calling all over the country and haven't found one for sale. I can't believe you found one!"

"The car's in Detroit. It may have a few miles on it, but don't worry about it. I'll have it driven out here."

So he jumped on it. I asked him to come by the lot and give me a good deposit and sign the papers.

When he came in, I had him sign an application for a title form. I used the same procedure I'd developed when a friend who left his Ford with me died. I sold it to someone and just wrote it up as a new car sale, ignoring the previous registration.

I wired Wild Bill $1,000. He said he liked the car so much he and his old lady were going to drive it up personally. I sent him the good plates and paperwork to avoid any problems with the cops if the car happened to be stopped.

When Wild Bill arrived, we had a hell of a party. I had the car detailed, waxed and delivered the next day. All went well, and Bill and his lady went to the airport to go home.

The next week, my phone was ringing off the hook—the triple black guy had told all his friends, and I had to do some thinking.

Les with Troy and Tracy during his auto theft years.

29

Les and brother Rob 1973

I went to my boss, who owned Cadillac Square, and told him, "I have a line on a couple Eldos to bootleg. How mad are you going to be if I make some sales?"

He said, "More power to you. I can't get any more anyway." He really didn't mind, but of course he didn't know they were stolen either.

By then, the triple black guy had gotten his paperwork from the state and all was well. The only problem with the whole thing was the numbers on the first couple of cars were just made-up typos on the VIN numbers on the title applications, but that couldn't continue. We had to come up with the numbers because someone was sooner or later going to have some warranty work done. In those days, you had a card with a metal stamp that you used for your warranty claims. The dealer would do the work, then put this card in a machine that would stamp all the info out so he could get paid from Cadillac. The Eldorados always had warranty work—the workmanship was terrible.

We started buying a lot of two- to three-year-old Cadillacs from Detroit new Caddy dealers and had them shipped to Seattle. We sandblasted underneath the chassis, gave them an undercoat and polish, then detailed them to look like new. We bought ten to fifteen cars a month from this one dealer, and they always treated us right. We gave the used car manager fifty dollars a week under the table for selling us the pick of the lot. I managed to talk my boss into letting me go back to talk to this guy since we'd only talked on the phone and nobody had ever met him. I went back to try to find some limos, Eldos and older convertibles and so forth. Well, that was for the company. What I really wanted was numbers to put on the cars I was selling. Jackpot!

Detroit was like the movies; it's all who you knew and how much money you had. This guy told me he could get warranty cards from the factory for cars that'd never been sold—damaged, wrecked, used for tests etc., no problem—for $100 each. I told him I wanted all he could get!

I took this information to my lawyer, who happened to be the ex-federal district attorney, and I told him the whole story.

Les's Porsche.

He was amazed and couldn't see what could go wrong. Now we were really rolling! I had cars coming in from California and Nevada weekly, and I was making $30 to 35 thousand a week. Of course, I was a big shot then!

I had a fight with Joan and ended up moving out. To "celebrate," I bought a Porsche, a Cessna, a drag boat, some motorcycles and threw some money down on a penthouse.

I had two great years of that before the hammer came down. I was charged with transporting stolen vehicles. Everyone was stunned. They just thought I was a good car salesman!

Les was sent to jail just after his mom died in 1968. The authorities let him come to his dad's funeral in September of 1969. After I was born, my parents took me to visit him at McNeil Island.

The Start of a Career

*A*fter Joan left him for his wrong-doings—taking the children with her—Les moved away from the Seattle-area and settled down in eastern Washington. There he met Linda, and they soon got married. They lived out in the country on a nice-sized piece of property that Les purchased to build a house and start a new life.

This time, life was going to be normal.

This time.

About two years after I got out of jail, around 1975, I was living in eastern Washington and building a house with my second wife, Linda. A friend from prison, named Fat Joe, showed up with a new rental car and lots of pocket money. We drank beer and told stories for about a week. He told me he'd just robbed a bank somewhere in Seattle and wanted me to go with him to do another. Of course, I said that there was no way I was going to do something that stupid. He kept hammering away at me over the beers.

The fact was, I needed the money to finish the house. Linda was working, but the house was costing way more than we thought it would. There was no well dug on the property. We hadn't even thought of that when we bought it. That was going to cost about five thousand dollars. The pump was going to cost another four thousand dollars, and then we needed a pump house, wiring, etc. Linda and I had been hauling water every day for the past year into the house, and it was getting damn old.

Joe finally broke me down to the point that I would go look at this bank he had picked out in Olympia. So we drove over through Seattle in his rental car to take a look.

After we checked out the bank, I realized I didn't like it, but the getaway was what sold me on the idea. All I had to do was stand by the door with a ski mask and he would do everything else. The plan was to rob the bank that was in a mall, and we would never leave the area. We would simply drive around back, go through a fence, down a gully and up a little hill to another part of town with the rental car parked right there.

The night before the robbery, we stole a van from the Oyster House and drove it to the bank. There was a laundromat next door to the bank that we went into to put on our ski masks and gain our composure. Then, we walked around the corner and into the bank lobby. I stayed at the door, scared to death, but I knew that if I saw any cops coming, I could be out of there extremely fast. Joe ran behind the counter, got the money, and we ran out.

We ran through the laundromat to the back door exit, jumped into the van and drove around the back of the mall. We parked the van and ran through a hole in the fence. Down in the gully there were some kids smoking pot, and as we ran by, they looked up. I'm sure they wondered what the hell was going on. We ran up the other side and to the car, and drove away. It all happened very fast. We headed back to eastern Washington, but stopped in Spokane, where we counted up the money. Once we split it, I had almost $15 thousand! I bought Linda a car to go to work in, since we only had the pickup. I had been taking her to work or I was without a car for the day.

Linda and I now had the money to complete our well, and we had running water again in our life. The Olympia Job point-

The Start of a Career

ed me in the direction that I would continue for nearly twenty years.

I never did do another job with Fat Joe, since the money lasted me for about six months. By then, Joe was long gone. It did give me a lot of time to think about obtaining more money that way, but I wasn't about to continue robbing banks with guns and ski masks and all the fuss that it caused. I needed my own bank robbing theory.

Over a six-month period in 1975, I developed my new action plan that included a police scanner. I thought that would be a wise investment, so I could know what the police would know at the same time. My approach in the bank wouldn't be with the tellers because if I was going to do this, I wanted as much money as I could get out of the place. During this time, another friend of mine, named Bo, got out of prison. He was much more level-headed than my friend Joe was. He also didn't like the bank robbers whom we met in prison. So we talked.

During our discussions, we managed to generate ideas that were completely different from anything we'd ever heard. It was groundbreaking! We chose an isolated bank in Bremerton, Washington, one that most likely had never been robbed before. One drawback was that the bank was a hard place to leave if the police were really looking for you. We needed a getaway car, so we stole a red one, drove it to Bremerton and left it there. Then we returned to Seattle and bought a pair of matching gray suits with the same black boots and gloves. Since we were close in size and stature, we looked very similar. We then rented a cabin cruiser from a boathouse in Tacoma. I'm an experienced sailor and waterman, and steered the boat up to a little inlet right down the way from the bank and tied at a nearby pier. At about eleven a.m., we walked from our boat to the car we had previously left waiting for us at the "Boat Bank." I thought that name had a nice ring to it.

Wanted: Gentleman Bank Robber

It was Monday before noon, and the bank traffic had died down real nice from the ten a.m. rush. We walked in and Bo went behind the counter. I went to the manager's office and brought him to the vault. Everyone was very cool, not doing anything but watching. We filled up a big bag of money and walked out of the bank, got into the red car and drove to the main intersection and turned right. We got in the left lane, turned into the parking lot of a mall, got out, and took our coats off and put them into the bag with the money. We took off from there on foot, crossed the road and walked down a little embankment to the boat. We slowly motored away from the dock and turned for Tacoma.

The police were going crazy looking for the red car on the highway. Finally, they figured we wouldn't drive it too far, so they started looking for it near the bank. They finally found the little red car. We heard on the scanner that someone told them we had gotten into a green Mustang. We listened to the scanner all the way back to the marina. We docked the boat, put the key in an envelope and dropped it in the mail slot with a note of thanks. Then we got into Bo's car and drove it to the Washington Hotel in Seattle, where we had made reservations. We sent for room service, cracked open a bottle of bubbly and counted the money—$94 thousand! That was it, and we knew we were on to something.

When the five p.m. news came on, we saw that the whole Seattle police force, shotguns at the ready, on the dock waiting for this fictitious Ford Mustang to come off the ferry. The next day, the Boat Bank Heist was on the front page of the *Seattle Times*. We managed to make a huge fuss that day.

Bo and I bought a motor home, and we took off perfecting our method of bank robbing, doing it better and better.

We went from coast to coast robbing little banks in towns like Clear Lake, Houston, Texas, Bend, Oregon and others, that we had a pretty good idea had never been robbed before. We

36

netted $48 thousand in Clear Lake and $68 thousand in Oregon. We even bought a safe-house condo in the Houston-area and furnished it. We purchased a new Ford and kept it in the garage. It was our getaway if something ever went wrong.

One day, Bo was already at the condo, and Linda and I showed up in our motor home. Bo had bought a new LTD that was all black, with leather interior. He had been trying to get next to the pair of airline attendants who lived upstairs. After spending money and taking them out to dinner for a month, he finally figured out that they were gay. When I showed up, he immediately wanted to go to work.

That's when we did the double bank job in Baton Rouge.

When we got back to the Houston condo, Bo's wife called and told him to get back home. His parole officer wanted to see him ASAP, so we rushed him to the airport. He went off with a nice carry-on full of money. Linda and I closed up the condo, put the car away and headed home. We never needed the place really. Later, in a nice gesture, Bo ended up giving all the furniture and stuff to the airline girls upstairs. Bo drove the car off and never came back.

I settled back down with Linda in eastern Washington and continued to build our house. I was still on parole at the time for the earlier stint of interstate transportation of a stolen vehicle, and I found out that I was going to be indicted again for another charge in Spokane, Washington. I had a lawyer there named Mr. Raymond Tanksley. He looked into the charge and confirmed that there was this truck in Alaska, and the authorities seemed to think that I stole it and took it to Alaska to work on the Alaskan Pipeline. Tanksley was right. Which meant I needed to go to Alaska.

Back in my early automobile days, my friend Butch, from Colorado Springs, Colorado, and I were partying with some Alaskan idiots who lived in the bars in Fairbanks. They told us about how the companies working on the pipeline needed all the

the edge just as it hit. It was a huge splash! That was one problem solved!

With the truck gone, we went back to Fairbanks, returned the car, got drunk and flew home the next day to Seattle. I then drove home to eastern Washington.

When I got home, I was so proud of myself. Linda told me lawyer Tanksley called and was wondering where I was. I'd missed a court appearance.

Thinking that the FBI would surely find out that they didn't have any evidence for a trial, Linda and I went to Hawaii with some friends, and I forgot all about the court. I figured going to Hawaii was a reward for me for finishing my parole, since you can't do any traveling while you're on parole.

In celebration, Linda and I bought a house on the beach for the rest of the summer and through the fall when it would have been bad weather back home. But when we returned home, I got arrested at the airport. There was a warrant out for my arrest for the court date that I missed. I was supposed to meet Bo for some more work. Jail time broke up the game.

The judge gave me thirty-six months for not appearing. While I was behind bars, Bo went broke and went back to the same bank we robbed the first time. He must have talked to the wrong person, because the FBI shot him dead as he came out of the bank with a bag in his right hand and his wig in the other. Not one warning shot. I read about it in an article in the *Seattle Times* in 1977.

I was first sent to McNeil Island, tried to escape and then was sent to Lompoc. I tried to escape from there and was sent to Leavenworth. After about nine months in that hole, and two months left on my sentence, the mailman gave me a letter. It was a copy of a letter the prison had sent to the state of Oregon, telling them I was going to be released on April 4, 1980. *Damn, after all of this, what was this about?*

The Start of a Career

I sat in my cell stewing on this. It dawned on me that one letter deserved another. Leavenworth's print shop did most of the printing for the prison bureau, so the next day I went down and saw some friends. I managed to get all the stationery for a letter with the words of my choosing: "Be advised, due to disciplinary conduct, Mr. Rogge will not be released on April 4, 1980 but on April 14, 1980." Of course, Oregon never followed up on the letter, and on the fourth, they were nowhere in sight and apparently planning on picking me up on the 14th. The warden didn't like it, so he had the guards deliver me to the Leavenworth County Jail instead of releasing me. It was an old wooden jail across the street from the little courthouse, and I was the only one on my floor. I did have a telephone though. I called everybody: Jeannie, Linda, Rob—anybody I could get a-hold of. I also wanted a lawyer; this wasn't legal!

Finally, that afternoon, I got them to take me in front of a judge who really didn't seem to know where he was—let alone the law. He said, "If Oregon isn't here by Monday at noon, I'll let Mr. Rogge go."

The only problem was that I knew Oregon would be there by Monday. I was sure the prison warden had called and, I think so did the judge. So, back to jail I was going to go.

The judge set a bond of some amount. Kansas is one of only a few states where you can bail out on extradition charges—it goes back to the slave days when run-away slaves were arrested and could get out if they had money and could run again. So I started into the phone, and I called everyone I could think of including my sister and brother—everyone I had a number for. By late Friday, I was down to calling Wild Bill, my friend from the car deal days.

He was broke and on heroin. Wild Bill said, "I don't see how I can help."

I told him, "You owe me! You need to find me a way out here—and fast!" Then I hung up.

Worry, worry, worry was all I did that Sunday night.

About eight o'clock, I heard the old guard coming up the stairs. I was the only one in that section of the jail, so I knew he had something for me. He opened the creaky old cell door and said, "Rogge, get your stuff. Bondsman's here."

All right! I was really ready for whatever was going to happen! Downstairs we went, and there was my friend Wild Bill!

Now, you have to visualize this picture: He had on a new suit that was two sizes too small; an obviously new shirt which had never been washed, with a neck that was two sizes too big; and a snap-on bow tie that no one in their right mind would wear. He had a tattoo of a tear drop under one eye, and he was wearing some messed-up shoes. If there ever was someone out of character he was it—but he played it out real well.

He presented the guard with some official-looking paperwork and said, "Sign here." When the old man did so, Wild Bill handed him another sheet. "Here's your copy. OK?" The guard nodded. "Thanks. See you." And we walked out.

Out in front was a beat-up 1978 Plymouth sedan. I got in and he walked around. I noticed that all the wires were hanging down from the dash—it had been hot-wired! As we pulled out and tried to find the main street to get us to the highway he told me his story. He'd written a non-sufficient funds check for the airline ticket, broke into a bonding company in downtown Kansas City, lifted the paperwork out of a desk, shoplifted the clothes, stole the car at the airport and had ten cents to his name—but he was now my friend for life!

We got to a Holiday Inn, and I gave him a story that I would pay later or in the morning since someone sent me money via Western Union—perhaps Jean or Rob. So we got some beer, ditched the Plymouth and partied all night. The next morning, I bought him a ticket home and gave him as much money as I could and we rode to the airport together and said goodbye.

The Start of a Career

A couple of years later, I had another encounter with Bill. I was driving down the Pacific Coast Highway 101 off the coast of Oregon where the road sometimes hovers over the rugged cliffs and valleys. It was very beautiful. I discovered the town of Pacific City. It was a little fishing village with a big fish cannery that you could see from the car heading south. Something made me turn around and find the road down to the little city of maybe three to four thousand people—not big. As a boy growing up in Hoquiam, Washington, I'd seen a few big canneries like this and knew there were many people working inside. It takes a large payroll to support a large factory like that—and that meant a bank! As I drove through the town from the north, there sat the bank at the end of the street.

I went in to scope things out. It was a nice bank with all women, but it had the worst getaway. The only way back out of town was the street I was on, and to get back to Highway 101, I'd have to dodge left one block and head back up the hill. The Oregon State Police would be at the top before I could, every time.

Walking around, I noticed something interesting. The builder of the cannery must have done well because he built an airstrip between the cannery and the bank's back door! I was sure the bank had never been robbed seriously, other than perhaps a drunk or dope fiend wanting money from a teller. I was sure it hadn't been robbed using a getaway since there was simply no good way out. That runway was like a magnet to me, and I decided to go for it, even though I didn't have Bo. I needed someone other than Linda to move cars for me and help me steal a plane.

I called my buddy, Wild Bill. Of course, he was broke again and back in Long Beach. I wired him some money for airfare, and picked him up. We drove to Bend, in the eastern-central part of Oregon, which is on the other side of the Cascades and about 150 miles from Pacific City.

43

I hadn't been to the airport in Bend before, but Bo and I had robbed a bank there some time ago and found that it was a nice slow town. Bill and I found a nice little Cessna 172 to steal. I felt comfortable flying it since I owned one a few years before in Seattle.

Stealing a plane is easy because, except for the fancy ones, the doors only have a magnetic switch between you and starting the motor. Then there's the bonus of always-full gas tanks, because of the fear of condensation—water in the gas—which could be fatal. We ended up finding a plane, but the weather needed to clear, since I only knew how to fly in fair weather. I didn't have a lot of time to wait on the clouds, and I was a bit nervous about flying over the mountains. It had to be clear, plus my map was of the highways below. But on the appointed day, the skies were clear, and the flight over the mountains was spectacular—a bonus in the life of crime!

I stationed Bill on the ground in Dallas—a town relatively near Pacific City where we would hide the plane until the right day. We had a pair of handhelds that worked on the marine band, so we talked most of the trip.

Once we were set in Dallas, things got tough. The only way we could top off the tank of the plane was from fuel that came from a drum—it had to be hand pumped. We had to change the plane's numbers to a number we found in a trade-a-plane paper for sale. Bill ran out of dope and wanted to go back to Los Angeles to get some more—but that was out of the question. We ended up driving into Portland's seedy area and got more heroin. I was getting nervous. I didn't know how long the stolen plane would sit on that little runway without being noticed, so time was getting tight. I'd spent a couple grand already so far, and everything was costing more than it should.

We targeted the fifteenth of the month, since we knew that was payday at the cannery. Flying into the runway in Pacific City was a bit hairy as the wind was coming from the north by north-west and the landing field was north-south. Thankfully, I landed just fine and taxied up to the back door and put the hand brake on. Bill got out dressed real nice, and he walked around to the front of the bank. He had never seen the bank up close, only from the hill above on the highway, so he noticed nothing. Bill got all four of the ladies to go back to the coffee room, cut the phone line, and kept the manager in the hallway. He unlocked the back door to let me in and went back to the plane that was idling like a champ.

I took the manager to the vault, which was a big thing with stainless-steel doors and lots of little boxes.

I told her, "Open the big boxes!" But they were empty. "Open that one!" I said firmly. Nothing in that one, either. "Where's the money?" I asked.

"What money?" She asked.

"The bank's money—don't play with me!"

And that's when she told me, "This isn't a bank any longer, it is a credit union. We don't have any cash on hand today, just checks."

I looked around and felt like a stupid idiot. Things were different. There was no longer a bank sign with their logo on the wall. *Damn! How could I be so stupid?* Still in a daze, I went out the back door and to the plane. I gunned the plane wide open. I turned around at the end of the strip and turned into the wind. As we were speeding down the strip, we went right by all the employees standing outside, watching us fly off. It was tough telling Bill what happened, but he'd been through many things, and since we didn't rob anything it didn't feel like we did anything wrong.

Back to Dallas we flew. We set off a can of WD-40 with a rubber band holding down the button. That fogged-up the interior of the plane, removing all the fingerprints. We were off—but damned-near broke. I took Bill to the airport and gave him my last two grand and said goodbye.

I never heard from him again. Later, I tried to look him up in the Long Beach area. I found a beer bar he used to hang out in. A guy I met there said Wild Bill got caught at the Mexican border coming back in a flame-red Cadillac Eldorado with the top down, a nineteen-year-old blonde hooker and a kilo of heroin in the A/C duct! Now that had to be federal, but I could never find him again, even with my prison contacts.

I had to make some money for myself after that. To hell with the fancy stuff—just a good old fashion bank robbery would be fine!

Learning to Run

Out of jail, thanks to Bill, but in Kansas City with only a few hundred dollars and no plan, I tried to get used to being free. I decided I would try Tucson, Arizona.

In my limited property I had a copy of my birth certificate and a letter from the Washington Driver's License Department. With some Wite-Out, a typewriter and a copy machine, I managed to make a license in a new name. I was sure by now Oregon had come to their senses and the old warrant had been updated.

Bless that sweet lady at the D.M.V. who said everything looked fine. Now please step over here for an eye test. Fifteen minutes later, I had a new I.D. in the name of Dan Shea.

I was doing well, and felt relieved that I could stand a police check. It was always a good feeling knowing no one wanted you for anything—I'd never been arrested with my new name. Although I had my license, I was still on foot; taxis were cutting into my limited funds.

I walked into a Ford dealership looking for a car to steal, and of course, a salesman came charging out trying to make a sale.

I replied, "Shit, no! I've got mine in the service department for the third time this month, and I'm waiting for that lemon now!"

The salesman slid away. I watched him return to the showroom where I knew he'd tell his co-workers "Don't mess with that one—he's upset!" Soon, nobody paid any attention to me, and I could just walk anywhere and sit in as many cars as I liked unmolested. Then I walked around to the back where the body shop was located, as well as all the demos.

Every car lot I've worked, the salesmen usually put the keys over the visor so others can show the cars as well. This was a fairly big place, and there were five or six cars parked back there. All of them had dealer plates, with the dealer's number on them— which was very problematic for a stolen car report. I spied a converted van with a television and all the goodies. It even had a bed of sorts if I had to sleep in the back. I decided that was the one, but I still had to have paperwork. So back to the showroom I went. Most of the salesmen had little cubbyhole offices, and I asked to use the phone in one that was empty. "Sure but dial nine first!" the guy said. I rummaged through the desk and grabbed a handful of blank contracts—and lo and behold, I got some rental agreements, too! Home run! I put the papers in my shirt and walked out the back to the van. I looked around, and still nobody was paying any attention. I fired up the van and pulled right out the driveway, headed off on the Kansas Turnpike.

Out from under a twenty-year sentence, I had good, new I.D., the van was going to be cool for a long time after I made up some papers to put in the glove box, so life was good!

Some time later, I picked up a hitchhiker who was going to Wichita, and we got along well. He was going to get a license to drive a cab. Now, I'm always interested in getting licenses—in my line of work I couldn't have too many I.D.'s. He told me to go to the bus yard and for fifteen bucks I could take a driving test and get a chauffeur's license. So I took him there where we both took the test, paid and drove the van around to get another Kansas driver's license. I was beginning to really love Kansas! I ended up getting another four more licenses for future use.

After getting our licenses, I took him down to the cab company where he was planning to meet and work for the owner of Best Cab—a really nice black guy who asked if I wanted a job, too. I told him, "What the hell," even though I knew nothing about Wichita. He gave me this little map and told me that the dispatcher would always help out. Here was the deal: I rented the car for thirty-five dollars for twelve hours; at the end of the day, I had to give twenty-five bucks to the dispatcher; I bought the gas and kept the rest. He said if I drove hard for twelve hours I should be able to keep $100.

I told him, "I need a place to stay."

He looked out the window. "I saw you was driving a new fancy van. Didn't figure you needed a place to stay."

"I just got out of the Navy."

So he called a couple places and found a furnished apartment down in town in an old hotel. If I moved right in, then he would vouch for me. *Cool. What the heck,* I thought.

I was a little nervous, but he put me in a cab with an old drunk who'd been driving for years. After the first day, I tried it on my own. I got lost and didn't make a dime. Eventually, I figured it out. I met so many different people—if I just relaxed and didn't sweat the small stuff, it was fun. My overhead was very small, so I saved up some money. I could've just left, but it all was working out just too fine.

I got tired of driving his junkers that didn't get any mileage, so the owner took me to an auction where I bought my own car. He paid for the black and white paint job, and put a radio in it for me. I had my own legal car that I could drive almost anywhere in town, and no one paid any attention to me. I could work any hours I liked.

In July it was around 110 to 115 degrees in the day. But after the sun sank, it was real nice, so I drove from seven p.m. to whenever. I met drug dealers, hookers and all types of interesting people. I would drive until I cleared the $100, then head home. After some time, I had regulars. My car had a number that was real easy to remember (although I can't remember it now). The dispatcher was really cool and would call me at the apartment if something good came up, since I dressed nice and my cab was a couple of notches above the rest. I hardly used the van at all.

One day, I was downtown going up an alley to get somewhere faster, and an armored truck pulled in front of me from nowhere. Ever notice how these assholes always assume they have the right away? They stopped at this little area with an unused loading dock. Of course, I was always looking for a money angle, so I went around the block to see what was in front, since there were no clues from the back. It was a long skinny bank in the middle of the block. I noted the time, even though I wasn't usually up at this time of the day—but I would be now!

Over the next few days, I parked downtown in the cab zone and watched for the armored truck. I came to watch on Monday, Wednesday and Friday at about 10:30. On one of my surveillance trips, I noticed there was a plain steel door on the loading dock—and it had been left open! I put my silly taxicab hat on, grabbed my clipboard and walked into the long hallway. The first thing I saw was the manager's office, then down the hall there were two more little offices, then the lobby. Then I went back out.

I had to know what they did with the bags that they left, so I walked in the front and asked for the person who called a cab, all the while looking to see what they did with the bags. I couldn't see where they went, but after some time I saw the bags in the hallway when they were leaving. Where did they come from? I could see the vault. It was in the front right side of the bank, clearly visible from the street, so the bags didn't go in and out of the vault. For a week, I kept going in the bank to see if I could figure out where those money bags were coming from. I was sure they thought it was strange someone was calling a cab a lot! Then I finally saw them come out of the last office—home run!

I went back to tidy up my rent and to tell the cab guy I had a death in the family. That done, on Wednesday at 10:30, I went back and parked the cab at the end of the alley, 150 feet from the back of the bank. The door was open like before, so I just walked into the office where the bags were lying on the floor next to this guy's desk.

I pointed at him as he looked up, and said, "Let's not make this a homicide!" He shook his head, scared. I picked up a bag in each hand. I always wonder why people don't realize if both my hands are full, where's the threat?

I walked out of the bank door as calm as could be, popped the trunk, (cabs always have an easy way to open the trunk), threw in the bags, drove to my apartment building, called the dispatcher to tell him to have someone pick up my car keys that were over the car tire until I could get back, filled up the van with the little bit of stuff I had and headed to Tucson $37 thousand richer. Life was good!

You might wonder why I was driving a stolen van with cash to buy something else. Well, I liked the van, and I'd gotten a new set of plates for a rental van from behind the counter at the airport one day. No one was at the counters when there were no flights coming in, and the cabbies used their phones while they were waiting. It was an easy thing to take them. So with that, and after six months of washing it, the van certainly felt like it was mine!

I went in high spirits, and in the best shape I'd been in since I left Leavenworth. I picked up another hitchhiker along the way since it was getting lonely. The guy's name was Steve, and he was down-and-out, looking for work and running from who knows what. We got along well, so he hung around.

When we got to Tucson, I called an old friend who was working his ass off as a welder. He was happy to see me—much to the chagrin of his wife. They knew someone who had a furnished trailer for rent that was pretty cheap, so Steve and I moved in. I parked the van in a long-term parking place next to a mini-storage, and bought a ten-year-old Oldsmobile to drive during my stay.

Steve didn't have any money, and he wasn't looking too hard for work. He knew I had some money since I was paying for everything. A month or so went by, and we were having a good time. I went out one night with my friend, and Steve stayed home. We had a few beers, then he took me back to the trailer. I noticed the Oldsmobile was gone. I thought Steve probably went out for something, but on a funny feeling I looked in his room. All of his stuff was gone. I was really worried now. I dragged the refrigerator into the middle of the kitchen to look for my money that I'd hidden behind it. Gone! He'd cleaned me out! Damn! I had about ten bucks in my pocket. Steve must have figured out I had some money stashed in the trailer somewhere and he had hours to find it.

Now I was in bad shape with no money. It was time to go back to work—only one of my rules was never to work under the pressure of being broke if I could avoid it. I couldn't avoid this one.

I borrowed some money from my buddy. I finally found an old Camaro parked in front of a house. The keys were in it, so I hopped in and twisted the starter. The goddamn thing was missing a muffler or something because it sounded like a B-25! I pulled away—somehow, nobody noticed the commotion—and drove to a gas station for five bucks worth of gas.

The next step was a bank on 22nd Avenue I had been looking at since my arrival. I was really worried about the getaway. The car wasn't reliable—I was afraid to turn it off. The one thing I had going for me was I still had a scanner—Steve didn't take that. As I sat with the bank manager waiting for the vault clerk to come back with the money, I kept looking out the window at the radio antenna on the car. That piece of shit jiggling back and forth was my assurance that the engine was still running. Had it died, I doubt it would have started again—and that would have left me in a pickle! But soon the girl came out with three canvas bags—unaware of the bag I'd brought—I just took them and walked out the door.

I got in the junker and drove about ten blocks to the back of a deli parking lot. The scanner started squawking about the robbery as I was parking. I stuffed the bags in a shopping bag, got out and walked to my trailer with no problem at all.

Back in the money! It felt good to go from ten dollars to $40 thousand and home with no sweat.

The bank bags were tan canvas with the logo of the bank, so I had to get rid of them. I cut them up in to strips and flushed them—and ended up plugging up the toilet. *Shit! The plumbers are going to love this one!* After about an hour of sweat and a coat hanger, I got them out and went down the street until I found a dumpster. I never had canvas bags again. Stopping up the pipes would have blown the I.D. that I used to rent the trailer, and that wouldn't have been good.

When my friend came home from work, I talked him into taking a couple days off to drive me to San Diego. It didn't take much convincing, as he was working in that heat welding all day, and was almost burned out. Plus I gave him $4 thousand and my favorite van to take me there.

I have always loved cars, and I can usually spot a nice car a long way off. Coming into San Diego we went down used car row—just used car lots with no dealers but medium priced cars. I caught sight of a three-year old Fleetwood Cadillac. It was bronze with a round padded top that was Cadillac's best four-door with little tables in the back of the front seats and the works. We circled the block and went back. The lot was closed and had a fence around it with an emergency phone number on the gate. I copied the number down, and we found a nice motel right on the beach at the bay. We both had friends there, and it was party time right on the beach.

The next day, I called the phone number of the lot. It was run by one man who told me all about the car. He wanted $10 thousand for it, so we took it for a drive. It was perfect, save for one hubcap that was painted to match the car. The owner said he had it; it was bent but could be fixed. We settled on $7,800 with no sales tax, and he just gave me the title—leaving it in the last owner's name.

After a week, my friend went back to work. I headed up the coast to Bellingham to see my kids, Troy and Tracy. I hadn't seen them, or their mother—my first wife, Joan—in about four years. When I lived in eastern Washington with Linda, my second wife, we had them for the summer, and Joan, a Realtor, had them for the school year. Joan hated me. I treated her real bad while we were married, so I guess I don't blame her. I was too immature to raise children. Being a family guy just got in the way of the hedonistic lifestyle of a bank robber. So I planned to buy my way back into her good graces.

On my way north through California, I stopped and saw friends from the Navy living in the state. I told them of my predicament. We came up with the idea that I needed a front—other than just retired—and somewhere the idea of jewelry salesman came up. It sounded good to me. The cheapest jewelry was the Indian silver rings and such, but I wanted something with a bit more class. I decided to take a quick trip to New Mexico, and had fun buying a load of silver stuff with a nice traveling sample case. While I was there, the jewelry shop owner told me of an Indian lawyer in Albuquerque's Isleta Indian Reservation I might want to meet if I was interested in really good stuff. When I got checked into a motel, I called him and was told to come over. His specialty was gold and turquoise rather than silver. He turned out to be really nice and took me to his workshop. His collection was simply gorgeous—mostly rings and bracelets. When it came to the price, he simply weighed the jewelry. Since the price was very good, I bought almost all he had—now I had a case full of beautiful jewelry to show. I had some business cards printed up, so my story was nice and strong.

When I got up to Bellingham, it was getting close to Christmastime. But Joan wouldn't let me see the kids. I had brought gifts to buy my way back into their hearts, but it didn't work. I was really disappointed. I'd really wanted to see them. But I kept moving on.

I called Linda since I was in the region, and she was happy to hear from me. Her family had pressured her to divorce me while I was in Leavenworth. Her dad was an ex-sheriff who never liked me and wanted me out of the family. So we decided to go to Vancouver for the weekend, but we took separate cars just in case.

Back in the early 80's, driving to Canada was very easy—you stopped, told Customs the purpose of your trip, and being a U.S. citizen, you had a good time. Linda was ahead of me and went right through. I hadn't given any thought about the California tags on my car with my Kansas driver's license, but because of them, I got a more thorough review of my purpose of visit.

I told them, "My ex-wife and I just want to spend the weekend together."

The Customs officer asked, "What do you do for a living, sir?"

"I'm a jewelry salesman."

"Do you have any firearms with you, sir?"

"No," I said.

"Do you have a sample case along with you?"

"Sure do. Interested in some gorgeous Indian jewelry?"

"No, sir, but you'll have to leave that in the bond shop."

I didn't want to leave all that stuff somewhere, but I said, "OK."

"Are you sure you don't have any firearms, sir?"

I *did* have a pistol in my briefcase, but he'd already told me I had to go back to the bond shop, so again I said, "No, officer."

His eyes got hard and he asked me, "Would you please step out of the car?"

When I did, he asked me to open the trunk and the case. The gun was wrapped in a facecloth inside my attaché case. He went right to it. He motioned for me to step back, grabbed the gun, popped the clip out, and stuck the gun in his belt. "You're under arrest and we're seizing your car." He took me into the station, made a call and had Linda stopped somewhere up the highway.

Shit!

The Customs guy was very nice about the whole thing, and I asked him, "How did you know to go right for the gun?"

He said, "I put together the California tags and the jewelry salesman. Every jewelry salesman traveling in the U.S. always has a gun!"

Dumb me! At least my Kansas driver's license held up. Just then, Linda was brought in. We hadn't been together two hours and already I'd gotten her in trouble with the police again!

They put us in two different rooms, but our stories checked out. After about twenty minutes, the Customs man came to us as we were sitting on a couch together and told me, "Here's the deal. You can continue into Canada, and stay for seventy-two hours. Your car has been seized, but it can be re-claimed for $400. Same with the gun. You can take the jewelry back to the U.S.-side when you head back."

I told him, "Keep the gun, it isn't worth $400, but I want the car." I didn't want them to arrange to hand the gun to the U.S. Customs. That was just asking for more trouble and delays.

"OK," he said, and gave me some papers to sign for the car.

I paid the $400, got into my car and finally took Linda to Harrison Hot Springs.

Coming back I picked up my case, kissed Linda goodbye and headed up to Montana.

The FBI slowly began to realize there was one bank robber responsible for a slew of unsolved heists on their books. What they weren't sure of was his identity—since he used so many. Because of that, they couldn't post his picture in the papers or on the television yet. They did have his fingerprints and that made Les vulnerable. Les was always good at creating new sets of I.D.—whether he made them himself with a copy machine or had someone help. He was always changing his identification, sometimes building up a few spares for the future. Les was aware that a simple traffic ticket could bring him down—an arrest with the subsequent taking of fingerprints would put him in a penitentiary for good.

Eastward on I90 going through the Rockies was so beautiful. It was cold and clear, and the only snow was on the side of the road. The scenery made you feel so good to be alive and without any worries. I'd had friends who knew what I did ask me, "How can you be a bank robber without worries?" Sometimes you just know when things are right. The stop at the Canadian border proved that my I.D. was good-as-gold, and the law knew nothing of who I was. Life was good.

I stopped for the night and got a good meal at a steak and ale restaurant with a bottle of wine, and I reflected on my diminishing cash reserves. I always tried to not go below $5 thousand— that way I didn't have to do things out of desperate need and could be more careful if things weren't going right on that day. There was always tomorrow. Obviously, it was time to get some more money.

Driving around looking for the D.M.V. to get some Montana tags for the car, I spotted a small two-lane drive-up only bank with two young ladies working the windows. I made a point to go back at night and look in the windows. What was interesting was what I couldn't see—no cameras! Inside was a very open area with two drive-in lanes on one side, a door with a peephole in it, and outside was a parking lot for about four employee cars, with the whole thing next to a small mall. There were two cars there during the day. Time to go listen to the scanner!

I found a little car auction place that was open on a weekend night, and these were great because I could buy a car with cash that nobody remembered as disposable get-away cars. I bought a white Nova, and put a couple of Radio Shack phony antennas on the car.

Most states have metal license plates, and Montana was no exception. I removed the plates and used a magnet on the back of new plates so it would just stick on. When I was ready to abandon the car, I would pop off the plates and throw them in the trunk. Nobody ever paid much attention to what I was doing.

I never missed a flea market either; the best were in California. On my last trip, I'd bought a couple of phony badges and a black case. A quick flip and it looked good to just about anyone. My hand-held scanner looked like a radio the police might use, and I had a clipboard with some blown up photos off a copy machine that looked like mug shots.

With my preparation complete and dressed up nice, I drove around the bank and through the drive-up lane—a little too far for a transaction but sort of in the way for the next guy. I walked up to the speaker, smiled and flipped open my badge. I showed the clipboard to the girl and said, "I have some photos of suspects in a check-writing scheme that I'd like to show you. Maybe you can help us." I motioned to the steel door.

Without hesitation she got off her stool and headed for the door. *Gotcha!*

Of course, she shouldn't have opened the door. She should have called someone to check the badge. But people are mostly embarrassed to ask for I.D. She just opened the door, and I stepped in. That's when I told her I was robbing her.

She kept saying, "Oh my God, I'm going to get fired!" I tried to tell her she'd been tricked—it wasn't all her fault. But she seemed unconvinced. Both of the girls were very cooperative, and I took in $85 thousand. I did really well in Missoula.

Finally, the FBI put together a case against Les and started exerting pressure through the media. He was featured in many newspapers across the country. In the Seattle Times *there was a front page collage of pictures of men they thought Les was. They said Les led a gang that robbed banks throughout the Northwest, using disguises that made them look Latino. Either the FBI had it wrong, or the newspaper was generating stories, or both, but Les never did lead a gang of more than he and a friend in his entire career. He also never used disguises to make himself look Latino, beyond coloring his hair. He'd robbed quite a few banks by this time, but some of the "jobs" he was accused of doing, he hadn't.*

Back on the highway with my bag a lot fatter than I was a few days previously, I went to visit Tim, from Las Vegas, an ex-con who I'd met in prison in the 60's. He'd been in for smuggling marijuana from Mexico, but he wasn't a criminal. He was just someone who loved to smoke pot. He'd married into big money; his wife's family owned a big company in Las Vegas, but as wild as it sounds, he had no idea about his new wife's background until they were married. They'd moved to Taos, New Mexico and I drove out to see him.

His wife, Lisa, was beautiful and very gracious, and really welcomed me, which was something unusual. I found most of my friend's wives didn't really take to me for fear that I would get them in trouble.

Of all the things that Tim had—a '57 Chevy that was so tricked out it must have cost $100 thousand, bikes, horses, trailers—he didn't have a regular car. Lisa started borrowing my Cadillac and fell in love with it, so I sold it to her. Then one day in Albuquerque, I saw an old GMC pickup. It was a special edition, straight but well-used—it was love at first sight!

Tim had just bought a seventy-five acre ranch in Reserve, which is down in the southwest corner of New Mexico, not far from Phoenix or Tucson. He wanted me to stay there and look things over while he decided what to do with it since Lisa didn't like it down there too much. It was too remote with no doctors for the kids, etc. So I took my newly-bought truck down with Tim following me, and it turned out to be a great place to hang out. It had a two-bedroom house, a huge open span building with a cement floor and came equipped with a 4500 Ford backhoe with a front loader. He had every tool known to man, and they were all brand new.

He introduced me around: there were two beer joints; one was a restaurant that cooked good steaks, and the other was just a country beer tavern. Then he went back up to Taos.

I spent a couple of months working on my truck, fooling around with the backhoe and the motor bike and playing with Tooker, the puppy Tim gave me for Christmas.

While I was up visiting Tim and Lisa in Taos, Lisa's sister, Mary, came out from Las Vegas to sort of dry out from the fast life of Sin City. We got along well enough for her to come to Reserve and spend some time. I enjoyed being with her, but she couldn't handle the no-people atmosphere and needed to be in a city. So with the truck done, we locked up the ranch, moved to Albuquerque and rented a condo. It had a beautiful view of the valley. One morning, we woke up to a sky full of hot air balloons, maybe a hundred of them right off our balcony!

It was October again and my money was low. With nothing else to occupy my time, I started looking for banks to rob, and in that city it didn't take long to find a few that met my criteria. I robbed three banks: the first was on Eubank Avenue that I stole $76 thousand from; the second was a credit union I stole $35 thousand from. The third was a fairly large bank on Montgomery Blvd with an alley behind. I parked Mary's Ford Ranchero at the apartment complex next door and just walked through from dropping off the getaway car to hers and drove away. Listening to the scanner for the next few hours at the condo it was apparent all was well, and I came away with $87 thousand.

Of course, I had changed the plates on Mary's car back to the correct Nevada tags. At first she didn't realize I had used her car. She suspected something, but thought it was a pot deal or something like that, since we all of a sudden had an in-flux of money. She had an allowance and had used that for the last month's rent, but after that I covered for her. It was a good time.

Then, Mary left me for Christmas in Las Vegas. I headed to Bellingham, Washington, to try to see my kids again, who were now close to their young teens, and give them some gifts I had purchased. I stopped in Tucson and purchased a new camper for my truck, and then went north.

Although Les wasn't close to his children, his son Troy believes that Les was watching him grow from a distance. Once, Troy got in a minor car accident. He got an estimate of $3,000 to fix the car and had no way to pay it. The following week, an envelope with no return address showed up in the mail with $3,000 cash in it. He *hadn't had contact with his dad in years, but somehow the exact amount showed up for him at just the right time.*

After a couple of days driving, I called Joan, while she was at work. When I arrived, she was angry and didn't want to have anything to do with me, nor would she let me see my kids again. I was so depressed. Although I wasn't there for them, I really loved them and missed them badly and wanted to catch up.

I took off for eastern Washington to check on my old house that I had built with Linda in Colville. I didn't know what had happened to the property since I had left many years ago. I had good feelings about visiting for a couple days before any rumors started to fly. I didn't want any police attention because my warrant from Oregon was still active from my last jail escape. But after a couple days in Colville, I started to hear rumors from friends of some heat developing and decided to head east to Montana. I always head the opposite way everyone expects you to.

This was the life of being a wanted criminal, and I was getting really good at it. I had been running from the police my entire life, and was now wanted by the FBI for about twelve bank robberies—or however many they connected to me—since my jail escape. My plan was to change the tags on the truck and get a new driver's license from one of my old Kansas driver's licenses that I still hadn't used so I had a good set of I.D. and stay ahead of my followers and fans.

In Missoula, I took the name of Donald Rose, and got a new title for the truck and camper. I spoke to my friend Tim in Taos and found out that I was hot—and not in a good way—in New Mexico. Someone had seen me change the tags on Mary's car after the bank robbery. The police contacted her, and they had my name and a description of my truck. But they didn't have the license number, so I did the right thing getting a new license and tags. The truck now had a camper on it, so I felt good about being in it.

After another long drive from the warm but green Northwest back down to the Southwest where the sculpted indigenous hills met the endless red-clay skyline. Tim met me at a car wash in Taos. "You can't come around my house anymore" he told me. We sat in the camper and had a few beers. I took off again the next day and headed toward the warmer and moist weather of the South. Without much of a plan, I wandered into Corpus Christi, Texas.

I had friends from Reserve that were working on Padre Island, so I went to visit them as they were living almost on the beach in a camper. Padre Island has miles of unspoiled beaches sitting beside the Gulf of Mexico under the sun. I rented a furnished condo on the second floor with a balcony in an almost empty gated community that was right on the water and settled in for a while.

In town, I found a Mexican auto shop that installed chrome roll bars and covers, and I had them put those on and a new tailgate on the truck. I really liked the look, so I sold the camper. While running some errands, I found a bank in nearby Seabrook that seemed to have good potential, so I directed my energy toward robbing it. It always seemed like when I ran out of plans I'd start thinking of banks to rob. Then with a case of money, things would seem to just come together. So I picked up my belongings and moved on.

Seabrook, Texas is about thirty minutes south of Houston, halfway to Galveston, and minutes away from NASA's Space Center. I rented a little furnished apartment and started to listen to the scanner to get the feel of the area. It was a transient type of area, with everyone coming and going. There were lots of flea markets: at one I picked up a county sheriff's badge and I.D. to go with it for thirty bucks; and there were all types of phony driver's license blanks, guns and everything else you could think of. I got a large collection of other forms for birth certificates, marriage licenses, voter's cards and a small Walther PPK 9mm that fit into a wallet for my back pocket. Some of those items traveled with me for years—fifteen years later, I still had the badge and the gun with some of the forms!

One day at a Sears store, I found a wallet on the ground with a dozen credit cards and everything a person would want for I.D. His name was Harry, and he was from the Houston area. The only problem was he was black and must have worked for NASA. In the wallet was a mini photo of a high school diploma, so with one of the phony driver's licenses that I got at the flea market that had my picture on it, and some skill with the copy machine, the new additions made for a real impressive flash of I.D. Of course, it wouldn't work for the police or someone who could run a police check, but everything else was as good as gold. I could rent a car, check into any hotel or motel; it was a great set of I.D. I used the wallet outside of the U.S. as well to cash hundreds of thousands of dollars of bank traveler's checks. The poor guy who lost it must have been contacted for the next fifteen years!

The bank I concentrated on was at Highway 146 and NASA Boulevard. It had about twelve employees, no guard and the manager was a woman—not one male clerk. I called the manager on the phone, using her name—which I'd discovered after doing my homework—and asked for an appointment. I said I was temporarily working at NASA, and needed a bank for business.

My getaway plan was to head to Clear Lake, a town that was about two miles from the bank. It was an unlikely direction of response from the bank alarm since it was mostly federal land in the area. The only area that would have a sheriff was Old Galveston Road at the far west end of that area. So even if the alarm was sounded as I left the bank, I could get there twice as fast as a sheriff's car could. I rented a small fishing skiff to take me to my truck on the south side of Clear Lake.

The manager was a sweet, blue-haired lady, who told me after reading my note, "I've been waiting for this day. I'll give you my total cooperation."

That fit my plans very nicely. I asked her, "Do you believe in the here-after?"

She said, "Yes."

"Because I'm here-after your money." For some reason, she didn't laugh.

I ended up taking the twenties, fifties and hundreds, along with two boxes of blank traveler's checks and a small bag of gold coins. I thanked her for her cooperation and walked out to the reliable—but piece-of-shit—car I'd bought at a flea market for $475, started it up and got on the highway. A few blocks down NASA Boulevard, I heard the alarm on the scanner—home free! I parked the junker in a lot right near the lake, which was sort of a scrap yard with nobody around. I set off a can of WD-40 with a rubber band to hold down the button that would fog the entire interior to prevent fingerprinting. Taking off my suit coat, I folded it with my shoulder holster, and stuffed it in with the money in my big bag. I donned a bright red windbreaker and walked down to the little boat that was tied to the piling and banging against the bank, stepped into the boat, tossed off the line, pulled the starter rope and was off. The scanner didn't have any more information other than the color of the getaway car—they still couldn't decide on the model. Life was good at that moment. The right amount of planning created a payoff worth $87 thousand, plus $48 thousand in traveler's checks and a handful of Krugerrands worth around $125 each.

Having money in my pocket always made my feet itch, and that night I headed toward Louisiana.

Judy

Heading east on I-10, I was just going to be going. I stayed in real nice hotels just thinking about what I wanted to do next. When you burn your bridges as you go, the only momentum is forward—good or bad.

One night, I stopped in Lake Charles, Louisiana, to eat and service the truck. That GMC was really a "looker"—in Fulton Beach alone it had almost been stolen twice. I'd bought the best theft deterrent system I could find, but a determined thief could drag it onto a low-boy type trailer and take it away. It wasn't just the truck I was concerned about—I'd hidden money in the doors, with spare I.D. and the works. I figured, if things went wrong I could get to the truck and start over. Because of all that, I was always worried about where I parked it at night. I found that the nicer the motel or hotel, the safer the parking was. At my motel in Lake Charles, the parking was out front. I sat on the balcony, smoking a joint and staring at the little red LED glowing in the center of the GMC emblem on the driver's fender, meaning the alarm was on. I felt so alone. Then, I remembered something about Lake Charles that was in my address book.

I rummaged through it and found a little note from my friend, Larry Henriksen, who I'd met in prison: "Call sister Judy in Lake Charles" at this phone number. Looking up somebody on the outside was something I almost never did. I wouldn't just

Judy

call people I didn't know from a number someone gave me in prison. But I figured I would take a risk, so what the hell?

The phone rang, so the number was good. Then a female answered the phone, "Hello?"

"Is this Judy?"

She was a bit hesitant, then said, "This is she."

I told her my name (which didn't mean shit, since it was fake), "Larry told me to give you a call if I was ever in Lake Charles." We talked for a while, and I asked her out to dinner. She said yes to the next night and gave me directions to her folks' property on Black's Bayou (which was the family name) where she was living in a trailer off the driveway.

The next night, I was kinda nervous. I hadn't been on a real date in years, so I dressed up and drove out there. The road was gravel that my truck didn't approve of. I drove slowly so I wouldn't kick up a lot of rocks. As I crept up the driveway, she must have been looking out the window, because she was at the truck door before I could get out. We went to a real shit-kicker country bar with live music. (She told me later that had been a safe place for her to go on a blind date.) We had a great time and ended at my hotel sitting on the balcony, talking and laughing until dawn. I told her I had picked up some new marijuana and could try it out, but it turned out to be a burn—nothing to it. We had fun anyway, and to this day she still says I tricked her to my hotel with the promise of good drugs! That was the first night of the rest of our lives—it's been almost three decades now with her beside me.

Judy had a little boy named Lee, in the first grade at the time, and after some time dating, we rented a small apartment together. Every day she took me around the town and showed me the sights. She was, and still is, a great teacher of the history of the South. She showed me things like the old statues in city squares that have their backs to the north—very interesting.

I got along great with Judy's folks. Her mom, whom I called Grandma, and her dad, Floyd, had a rule of no drinking around or in Grandma's house. Floyd called beer "strawberries" for some reason, and sometimes we would sit on the dock and drink, and throwing the cans underneath. The country is low-low, and it flooded all the time. Once, after the waters went down, the lawn was covered in empty beer cans—we both got a tongue-lashing from Grandma that day!

Floyd was almost legally blind, but he still managed to drive to the market for his "strawberries." The roads there are the tops of levees, so to misjudge the way is to be in a deep ditch which has seen alligators and snakes. I have no idea how he got there—some sort of bayou Braille system! Floyd would turn in the parking lot of the market and drive until he hit one of the large, yellow steel poles surrounding it. That was his parking place! Some days he would miss the driveway and end up in the ditch. That would result in some neighbor or friend pulling him out and steering him in the right direction. Needless to say, his truck looked like a meteor had hit it, but mileage-wise it hadn't been anywhere but to get those "strawberries."

Judy worked all different hours, and it wasn't unusual for me to be at the Black's helping Floyd with something during the day. One day, Grandma asked me to drive her to the bank because she didn't feel well. I got her big, beautiful Oldsmobile out of the garage and took her to the bank, which was sort of at the edge of town. It was a nice location with trees in a quiet part of Lake Charles. I sat in the car while Grandma went in. She took a half hour or so to do her business. As I sat there, I took in the entire scene. It was a nice size branch, all female, out of the way, in a very peaceful location. Grandma returned, and the bug was set—that was going to be the next bank for me.

Judy didn't know what I did for money. She knew that I'd been in prison, but didn't ask any questions. That's the way of

Judy

the real South, no busybodies. She thought I had a trust fund that sent me checks. As the checks weren't coming on a regular schedule she was soon skeptical, but still didn't ask. I told her we should go on a nice trip somewhere when school was out in the first of June, which was just around the corner.

The next day, I took a cab and went to Orange, Texas, about thirty-five miles into Texas. I spent the day walking around looking for a getaway car to steal. Later that night, I went back to a dealership that I had visited earlier. I had taken a set of keys out of a station wagon during the day that I could drive off later. Nobody noticed a thing. I took the car back to Lake Charles and put it in a hotel garage for safe-keeping and ready for action.

While Lee was at his last day at school, I robbed Grandma's bank for $85 thousand, and changed cars. I got back in plenty of time to pick up Judy and the suitcases, swing by the school and got Lee. We were on an adventure! We were hoping to find a sailboat in Florida and go to the Bahamas.

On the road on the second day, somewhere in Mississippi, we stopped for breakfast at a local greasy diner and got a newspaper. Looking through the ads, I found a fifty-foot houseboat in Jackson for $13 thousand—which was way cheap! So we thought, what the hell. Judy admitted that she'd been a bit hesitant about the idea of going out on the ocean since she'd never sailed before. I called on the houseboat and discovered it belonged to a college kid who needed the money, so we went up to see it.

The houseboat was on Jackson's Ross Barnett Reservoir. We met the kid and boarded. It turned out to be a very plain but nice boat. It could have used a coat of paint and new carpets, but it was sound, so I offered him $9,500. Afterward, I found out he was way behind in payments to a credit union where he owed about $8 thousand, so after the deal he pocketed $1500 for himself. He loved the idea of cash, and the entire thing took about one hour at the credit union.

That same afternoon, we moved the houseboat—since the credit union had stolen cash—to a little out-of-the-way marina with an amusement park with a water slide that Lee loved. He was sort of lonely since he didn't have any kids to play with, so he spent most of the day there while Judy and I cleaned up the boat. We put in new blinds, tinted windows and new kitchen stuff. The boat had a generator that supported an all-electric kitchen, and it was a one bedroom with a dinette that made into Lee's bed. After buying linen and all the house stuff we needed, we started taking it out to get the feel for it. A fifty foot boat with a big Chrysler V8 engine is not simple to maneuver, but we mastered it with some practice.

After a couple weeks, we found a trucker who could pick it up on a trailer and take it almost anywhere. We looked and looked at maps to decide where to put it in the water. We decided to be Huck Finns and take it down the Mississippi River—only we were aiming to go up it. Boy, we were naïve!

Greenville, Mississippi, had a levee that the trucker could back down to let the boat into the water and off the truck. It has Lake Ferguson and a yacht club, and the launch was a hair-raising event. Just looking at the ramp, you could tell the truck had to back down into an impossible slope and then the boat would slide right off the trailer before it got to the river. If it didn't work, the truck wouldn't be able to pull the boat and trailer back up the bank because it was so steep—so it was a one-shot deal.

Another problem was that since the angle was so steep, it would submerge the back of the boat before it could float on its own, and the engine and generator were in the rear ten feet! If water came in too fast, it could flood the engine and generator. Judy came up with the idea to duct tape all the engine hatches to keep the water out during those few minutes.

I swear the entire waterfront came out to see these stupid people sink their boat.

Judy

The truck driver and I had consumed a few beers during all the preparations to calm our nerves. He kept telling me the decisions were all mine and if everything went to shit he didn't have the horsepower to pull everything back up. The levee was cement, and at a forty-degree angle, and when wet, offered no traction.

It was afternoon, and we were keeping half the town from going back to work. I shrugged and told the driver: "So let's do this. Go slow until the stern touches the water, then quickly back down far enough to float the boat off the trailer—real easy like. The worst that can happen is the engine gets wet. Not really a big deal."

Very carefully, the driver inched the boat down the ramp. I started the engine as the boat touched the water, and threw it in reverse to get away from the trailer as fast as possible. It worked! Judy's duct tape saved the day and kept out the water. The crowd loved the drama and greeted the sight of the boat floating free with a round of applause. We tied up at the so-called yacht club and celebrated!

We got hooked up with power and water, and life was good. The club was having its weekly party, so we had a nice fish dinner and met everyone. We couldn't understand the reaction when we told people we were going to travel upriver:

"Good luck," some said with a laugh.

"You're taking the boy with you?" asked one.

"You're crazy," a guy said flatly.

"You won't make it," another said.

Not knowing any difference just made us smile. Despite their opinions of our plan, we were invited to the weekend parties that developed in the middle of the lake from Friday night to Sunday.

Our friend, Little David, also had a houseboat that was a bit smaller than ours, and he would anchor out in the center and all sorts of people would tie up to him. He was very happy to share the burden of being at the center of things, and the party was a great happening on Lake Ferguson. There were perhaps fifty small boats all in tow. On the lake there was waterskiing, swimming, diving, drinking, eating and smoking pot that went on almost non-stop to Sunday. The generator would run all the time for the air conditioning inside, and supply power to keep the beer cold. We made some very lasting friends at these parties.

The only thing that needed to be done to the boat was an overhaul of the generator. It was still running, but was worn out. We accomplished that with a crane by lifting it out and taking it to Memphis to the Kohler factory. It was returned in great shape in a couple of weeks. With that done, we were ready to leave. But every weekend brought another going-away party that left us in poor shape to leave on Monday, so we stayed.

It took us five months to finally leave. We managed to get a home school program for Lee. I sold my GMC pickup to a friend who fell in love with it in Greenville and we bought a Moped we could carry with us. I'd been told that, since the river was mostly for commercial use, there were few places to gas up for pleasure

Floating down the Mississippi on the houseboat. 1982.

Judy

Judy on a sandbar on the Mississippi.

craft. So I bought two fifty-five-gallon drums, filled them up, made a rack and placed them at the rear of the boat above and a bit forward of the engine.

We made our way to Vicksburg and got a river chart the tug boats use from the Army Corp of Engineers. It was a big book showing every turn and obstruction on the river all the way down to New Orleans, and it ended up saving our asses.

The Mississippi is a shitty-ass river that's never been tamed. The trip to the end in south New Orleans was about 650 miles of submerged dikes that didn't work, banks that had failed and a huge volume of water with all sorts of debris and shit that flowed at a rate that was very deceiving. That seemingly flat, calm river was moving downstream at somewhere between five- to eight-knots! A boat like ours with a top speed of about fifteen knots wide open was just an accident waiting to happen. It meant we were about to suck gas at a rate we had never seen before. You have to make enough speed going by the rudders to make them work, so with the current and your steerage speed there's not much room to spare. Now I understood the remarks at the first party: The reality is you do not go *up* the Mississippi River, you go down like Huck Finn. We learned this right away as we first pointed upriver and got almost nowhere. Quickly, we turned around for more going-away parties.

On the first day, Judy was on the roof sunbathing, and I was sipping a beer and listening to music just enjoying the trip. Suddenly, she started pounding on the roof. "You'd better come and look at this!"

To get on the roof, you had to use the ladder on the back of the boat—which was a trip that was about thirty feet away from the captain's chair. So I headed up to see what her concern was. What I saw made me holler, "Shit!" There was a little line of agitated water almost completely across the entire river. I ran back to the pilot house, cranked the wheel 180 degrees and hit the gas. The boat swung around and headed as fast as it would take us upriver. As soon as I could, I anchored.

What in the hell is going on? I grabbed my chart and opened it, really, for the first time. I wasn't in the River any more. That ripple was a submerged dike! I worked our way around the end, and we got by.

From that sobering moment it was no longer a relaxing party trip—I had to pay attention at all times. Getting the feel for the system of numbered curves on the charts in relation to

Judy

the actual bends made the day extremely stressful and full of action. I was on the radio talking hourly to the tug captains. Most of them couldn't believe we were traveling on the Mississippi in a houseboat, but some envied our experience and gave us great safety tips. It was a great way to learn from the pros who used the river daily.

Night traveling was simply not done. Every evening we had to find a branch somewhere where we could get out of the river traffic, because the tug boats, sometimes pushing unbelievable loads of barges, are the kings of the river, and they took up the entire river in some of the curves. Sometimes we would stop at night, and the banks would be beautiful pure white sand. Sometimes they were two feet of stinky grey mud. But we were doing something that very few people had ever done and were proud of it.

One day, I was listening to music and having a cold one, when the air conditioning quit working. *Funny*, I thought, *I just had the generator overhauled a few months ago.* Normally, in a power boat, the pickup tube for gas to a generator will be a little higher in the tank than the main engines, so if you were running out of gas you would lose your generator before you lost your main power—a little warning notice. I knew we weren't out of gas, because that morning I had filled the drums on the deck.

I yelled out to Judy to come down and steer so I could go back and open the engine compartment hatches that were on the deck behind the house part of the boat. I told her to just keep it straight down the river. I opened the port hatch and looked at the generator sitting there quietly. I reached over to where the electric fuel pump was mounted to feel if it was running. I saw no leaks anywhere, so I was wondering if the fuel pump took a dive. As I reached for the pump body, I noticed a bit of wetness. When I touched the pump itself, I bumped the power cord—and it sparked!

Poof! I had a fire, and I was standing chest deep in the engine compartment!

The closest fire extinguisher was on the other side of the boat, and I couldn't turn off the juice to the hot power cord that seemed to want to touch everything. I had two fifty-five-gallon drums that were half-full right in my face, and almost right above the fire, two seventy-five-gallon almost-full fiberglass tanks on each side of the engine room.

I thought, *This thing is going to blow sky high and I can't warn Judy.*

But reaction from who knows where took over, and I reached over to the big V-8 and tore the ignition coil wire out of the distributor cap so the engine would die. I ripped up my t-shirt and wrapped it around the fuel pump to try to put out the fire. Then I ran for the front to turn off the ignition. Judy was cussing me for stopping the engine since she couldn't steer. I turned off the ignition switch and raced back to reattach the power lead to the pump and restore the wiring on the distributor cap, since we were then drifting down the river.

I got the wiring together, tightened up the fuel filter under the fuel pump, which was the source of the leaky gas, and then went back to the engine room to restart everything. I took another look at the fuel pump to check for more leaks—the original leak could have made one hell of an explosion with a couple hundred gallons of gas! At the end of the day, I was exhausted!

Our first stop was Vicksburg, so we called ahead and had a gas truck meet us next to an old dock. They ran a long hose down to us, but there wasn't anywhere to tie up and go to shore.

The next gas stop was only about seventy-five miles as the crow flies, but 225 miles by the curvy river. Gas was always a concern. We also didn't have a small boat to go to shore in places that didn't have a dock, but we managed to get gas somehow.

Judy

At Baton Rouge everything we had learned thus far just fucking changed. Spanning the river, carrying Interstate 10 was a bridge that was built so ocean-going ships had to unload to their barges to continue the trip up the river. A fifty-foot houseboat isn't intended to mingle with ocean-going ships, and they were everywhere. Just trying to stay away from them was a full-time job.

We found gas again at a construction site on the river. We were told by a guy manning a shack on a barge, to "Just pull alongside and we'll fix you up!"

When we did, all these workers got into the act. They took over our coolers and filled them with ice, and tanked us up. We were permitted to stay against that rusty barge for the night. The work was going around the clock, and it was a very uncomfortable place. But it was welcome, since the trip to New Orleans was another 125 miles with no hiding places to stay the night on this stretch. So we banged against the noisy barge all night long, then took off at first light hoping to make it to New Orleans before sundown. We didn't have to get there, but we had to find a place to stay the night.

That leg ended up being better than the Baton Rouge leg, since the river was well-marked, and the ships had lanes to stay in. So we hugged the shore and stayed as far from the big boats as possible. Then we came to downtown New Orleans that had a lot of traffic, but we had a great view of the city that you would never see unless you were on the river.

Just past town, we had to swing off the river or head off into the Gulf of Mexico—which is no place for a houseboat. You can turn north and head into the entrance to Lake Pontchartrain, or keep right and go east on the Intracoastal Waterway (called the ICW) that runs from New York to Brownsville, Texas, for barges and yachts. Right at that intersection there was a fuel dock—the likes of which we hadn't seen since Greenville. I asked the old guy there if he knew of a marina—because we were ready to take a break! He told us about this place way off the charts, up the ICW.

After many faulty turns, we found the Gulf Coast Marina tucked way back up a cut to the main channel. They had a fuel dock, but no one was monitoring the VHF radio. So we just tied up until finally someone showed up. It was apparent they didn't get much traffic other than boats that stayed there, so we got a covered slip. And much to our delight there were only three or four boats that were live-a-boards. There was a nice restaurant, with the Chalmette Highway at the front, a mini-storage warehouse and three rows of docks. The town of Chalmette was just a dozen blocks down the highway that was wide enough to ride our Moped on the shoulder. We soon knew everybody around.

There was no boat repair, just the restaurant and docks. We were the first pier out from the restaurant. We were backed into the slip so our salon was out from the dock and had a real good view of most of the area. We camped there for the rest of the winter. It was a real nice and quiet marina... or that's what we thought.

One night late, I was watching television and smoking a joint, when I looked out the side windows and saw a few black figures in the shadows running down my dock toward our boat. I could tell they were SWAT team members with automatic rifles and the whole works. I thought, *Oh shit, here it comes!* and just sat still, frozen.

They disappeared behind our boat, and then there was a long, weird silence. Nothing happened. We had no window or view directly behind us from the inside, so I decided to face whatever was going to happen. I for sure wasn't going to run anywhere. So I walked out the side door and to the back of the boat, and I heard a boat roar out of the docks. *What the hell was that? They aren't coming for me?*

Judy

The next day, we found out that the Customs Department had a hideaway office in one of the mini-storage spots next to us, and they kept a boat on the end of the pier! They were going on a raid! Nice quiet place, eh?

Soon after that, a fisherman came in yelling about a body floating in the canal. All sorts of cops came, but couldn't find anything—the body was gone. Two weeks later, the same thing happened—someone spotted another body floating, and here come the cops again. That time they found a body that was half frozen. After a big investigation, it was determined that the corpse came from the nearby restaurant freezer—the place we ate at all the time! At that point, it was time to move on from that so-called quiet marina.

We decided to go back to New Orleans and sell the houseboat; maybe go for a sailboat this time. We rented a big Cadillac Coupe Deville by the week, and I started to go to work finding a boat and a bank or two to pay for it.

I robbed a bank in Lafayette, Louisiana, and got a dye-pack. That sucked. I had to wash all the money and didn't get very much for my effort anyway.

Next, I robbed a bank in Hammond, Louisiana, where four young ladies worked a college campus bank. It was sweet: Lots of parking, lots of folks walking in every direction, with no regular police; just had the campus cops without guns. My getaway car never left the campus. The rental car fit right in the faculty parking area.

I walked in and stopped. No manager. Where was the manager? I walked up to the counter and asked for her by name. It turned out she was eating lunch right behind the curtains. Saying I had an appointment, I walked behind them to a break room.

She was very nice when I told her I didn't want to interrupt her lunch hour. "Oh, no. Please have a seat and I'll put this away."

When she returned, I handed her my note, and let her read it carefully. I asked "Am I going to have any problems?"

"Not out of me" she stated.

"Good. Who is the vault clerk?"

"That would be me."

"Good. When we go back in there, your job is to make sure no one trips the alarm, and then we'll go to the vault."

She agreed, and we went into the vault with no one's suspicions aroused. As she was filling up my bag, I faced out to watch the bank. She dropped a packet of twenties worth about $1,000. She looked up, nervously.

I told her, "Don't worry about that." And I picked up the bundle.

She finished and stood up straight. "That's it."

She had one of those wrap-around dresses that crossed in the front and tied in the back, creating a big pocket in front. So I took the pack of twenties and slid it in that fold of her dress. I told her "Thanks. And this is for your trouble." Then I walked out to the car.

I've always wondered if she turned it in or not.

Going back to New Orleans, you drive under Highway 55 on the old Highway 51, right under the new road for most of the way. I saw one car the entire way. Most of the time in the rainy season the road was half-flooded, but it wasn't on that day. The scanner went off when I was well away from the campus and in the Cadillac. My getaway car had been a little white junker, so the Caddy was golden. All was well.

Judy remembers: We were staying in this hotel and we had $187 thousand in cash in a briefcase with us, which we hid under the bed. We partied that night and went to bed, got up the next morning and left.

We were about sixty miles down the road, when Les said, "You got the briefcase?"

I said "No, I didn't touch that briefcase."

Judy

"Oh, shit!"

We had to go another two miles before there was an exit to turn around. I just knew we were going to go to jail for speeding! I mean he floored it, and we were flying by people. You would think he was driving for his life. We got back to the hotel, and saw that the door was open with the maid cart outside. He parked, sort of at about thirty m.p.h. and sideways, and ran up to the room. The maid was in the bathroom, so Les ran to the bed and reached under. It was there! When he walked out, there was a huge grin of relief on his face. Man, I remember that road went on forever and you know that maid would have been gone if she'd found it. There was no way she would have turned that in.

We decided to continue with the sailboat idea—or at least I talked Judy into it by telling her it was as safe as walking on the beach. With happy faces and a briefcase of money, we put the fully-furnished houseboat up for sale with a broker on Lake Pontchartrain. We hit Highway 10 East in our rental car, headed for Tampa Bay where we thought there was a good chance to find our dream boat.

The first stop was back in Lafayette for gas. Sitting there was a '78 Cadillac Seville, backed up to the fence at the edge of the lot. It was in beautiful condition—dark brown with matching padded top and natural leather seats. I've always loved those models, sort of like a baby Rolls. I went in the station and asked the owner what was up with the Caddy outside. He told me it was a diesel that had a bad motor, and the owner wasn't sure about fixing it. Cadillac wanted $7 thousand for a new motor, and the car at best, even if the motor was good, was worth $5-6 thousand. He couldn't make up his mind about fixing it.

That year GM had sold that model with a piece of junk diesel motor called a throw-away diesel. It was a converted 350-gas engine, and you couldn't rebuild them, hence the throw-away. But I knew the way out of that mess, and I wasn't going to tell anyone.

The gas station guy gave me the phone number of the owner, so I called him and we came to the agreement of $3 thousand for the car as-is. The three of us checked into a motel. I got on the phone to the same people in Austin that built my engine for the pick-up, and sure enough, they had done three to four conversions on that kind of Cadillac. For less than $1,500 they would send me all I needed to replace the total motor using most of the old motor stuff like the starter, alternator, A/C and power steering. The only real problem was the exhaust, so I got back with the garage owner who was thrilled to put it together with me for $350. Austin shipped the new motor the next day, and two days later when it came, the old motor was out of the Caddy. I worked all night with many beers, and the car was ready for the muffler shop in the morning.

We turned in the rental at the Lafayette airport, and late the next day, we were back on the road with our new ride. The car turned out great, and it drove like new. I knew I could turn the car into a profit when the time came to sell it.

Sailing with *Mr. T*

In April of 1983, we aimed for Tampa in the new Cadillac. We searched the Nickel Want-Ad newspapers, boat trader and any other for-sale magazines for a sailboat. We found one that looked great, but they never answered the phone. We ended up in Clearwater, Florida, at a broker's office. He had just the right boat: the *Tambourine Man* was an older, immaculate 42' Cascade Sloop with a seven foot draft that was priced just right—and turned out to be the same boat we'd called on before. The boat sparkled inside and out. It looked like new even though the owners were living on it. It came with a hard dingy that also sailed. It wasn't loaded with electronics, but it had a diesel engine for the refrigeration, had self-steering, roller-furling on the head sail, and a boom reefing mechanism.

We took the boat for a sail—and instantly ran aground! The owner was embarrassed, but it was a point in our favor to get the price down, as we wanted a deep keel boat anyway since they sail much better. We wouldn't be sailing in Tampa anyway.

The owners were asking $95 thousand. I started negotiations by throwing in the Caddy. The owner said he wasn't interested, but perhaps his brother who owned a hock shop was.

We drove over to his brother's shop, and right away he said he wanted the Caddy. He told us all the details about the boat. The owner was a dentist who was pulling teeth on the boat and got caught for income tax evasion. He had to sell the boat or the I.R.S. was going to take it by the fifteenth of the month. He owed them $55 thousand.

Now we really had some ammo to deal with! We offered $60 thousand, knowing they would have to take it. Then we did a bit of pricing for the equipment that we needed to purchase, like a new main sail. We priced satellite navigation and other equipment, all while we were letting the doc stew.

The next day, they tried to up it $5 thousand, but we said no. Then they agreed to the $60 thousand, and I told them to give me a day to get the money. It was then we got rid of the broker who wanted eight percent. I wanted to buy the boat directly from the owner with no paper trail. I figured the broker might wonder about $60 thousand in cash with some in small bills. So we made a deal with the broker for $3 thousand in cash and he would step away from the deal.

I went into town and sold the dentist's brother the Caddy. He drove me over to the rental car place to pick up something to drive while we refitted the boat.

In a couple of days, I called the doctor and told him that if he would give me his address—they'd just gotten an apartment—I would come by and pay them. I always asked people if they wanted a personal check or cash—and most everyone said cash. The doctor was different though. No way did he want that much cash at his apartment! He asked if we could meet as his bank—I thought he meant he wanted to meet in the parking lot. I wanted no part of the bank because those were the cocaine days in Florida, and any transaction over $10 thousand had to be reported to the I.R.S. at once. Things weren't going my way.

I showed up twenty minutes early to make sure no one was parked around there that shouldn't be. When the doc and his wife showed up, I thought we could sit in my car, count the money and sign a bill of sale. But when he got out he said the bank president was waiting for us in his office. My heart sank, but I thought, *What the hell, I'll play along a bit longer.*

Sure as shit, the bank president ushered us into his big office. He didn't ask our names beyond the fake first names we gave him—and that's how I wanted it. He handed us some paperwork, then asked how we were intending on paying. "Cash" I said, as I put my attaché case on my lap and unload it on his desk. He called for a clerk and a counting machine. The lady came in with a counting machine on a cart and ran it through. All was well until the machine stopped and began to beep. She lifted a $50 bill out of the damn machine, and said, "It must be a counterfeit." But the president decided it was just worn out. Finally, the machine churned through the pile of money. The president handed me a $100 bill and said it was too much.

As the clerk was bundling up the money, she reminded the president that they needed to call the I.R.S. as required by the law. He told her to call.

Shit! We could've simply stood up and walked out, but that would have left $60 thousand in the bank. So I just sat there to see what would happen, since the I.R.S. couldn't just be in the neighborhood. I knew it would take some time, so I didn't panic. Judy squeezed my hand, so I knew she was nervous, too! It seemed like an hour before the lady came back in with some papers in her hand, and told the boss the I.R.S. was busy and for him to fill out the forms, blah, blah, blah. My heart rate went back to normal.

The president slid the papers over to me, indicating for me to fill them out.

I asked, "What're these for?"

He explained, "They're just to show that the transaction took place."

I asked him, "Well, since the transaction is between the doctor and this bank, not me and the bank, shouldn't the depositor fill these out?"

He thought about it for a second, then slid the papers in front of the doctor, saying "I guess that's what's right if the doctor is going to deposit the money into his account."

Second near-heart attack in one day! I scooped up the boat papers, stuffed them into my case and headed for the door with Judy right behind me.

We headed straight for the marina and told the office we were moving the boat. We left the car up in the marina parking lot to be retrieved later. We unhooked the power, water and phone cable, and Judy pulled up the lines as I fired up the diesel. We backed out of the slip in record time.

We headed straight across the Tampa Bay and ran aground thirty minutes into the trip. The boat swung around on her fin keel, and we managed to get off. I broke out the charts to find where the damned channel was and made our way to the marina without further problems. It was over. We got our boat, and nobody knew our names or who bought the boat. I found out later, it took the I.R.S. some three years to come looking for the people who bought that boat for cash.

Taking *Mr. T* across Tampa Bay after purchase. March 1983.

Sailing with Mr. T

We pulled the boat out of the water right away and painted the scraped-up bottom. It took a couple of weeks to get a new sail made, buy some radios and get familiar with our new home. Meanwhile, we stayed at a nearby hotel in St. Petersburg while we worked on the boat.

Judy recalls: While we were at the hotel, and had a few bucks to our name, Les decided to have some plastic surgery done to remove a distinguishing mole on his face that was prevalent in his wanted posters. So he found a doctor, and while he was at it, decided to get a little tuck under the eyes in hopes to bring back a few years.

As Les recovered from surgery he had bandages over parts of his eyes, and they continued to bleed. He had these bloody patches with dried blood running down his face. There was nothing else we could do besides sit around the hotel room smoking joints and drinking until he healed.

One day, there was a knock on our door. Les got up to answer it, and there was a cop! The pot smoke billowed out of the room, and there was Les with dried blood running down his bruised face, and he answers the door high as a kite. "Can I help you?"

The cop said, "Oh, sorry, wrong room," and started to walk away.

Les got pissed and said, "Hey, what are you looking for? You come bother me on my day off!"

Man, I turned gray that day. That kind of shit happened all the time!

Unfortunately the eye-tuck made him look younger, so he looked more like his wanted poster that used an older picture.

Back at the beautiful boat—which we nicknamed *Mr. T*—we met lots of people at the little marina. We got word that the houseboat sold. The money we received from that helped us load up our new home with a television, linen, tools, a second anchor and spare parts. We invested in the very latest electronic technology called a satellite navigator from Texas Instruments that was big, like a VCR player. It was the latest and greatest navigator—had to have it! It worked off of satellites and pinpointed your location, and with the sailor's biggest fear being "land is thy enemy," you could see where the land was before you hit it. So after five thousand dollars and the correct chart, it would show us where the land was and wasn't. The problem with the first machines was sometimes the satellites would bunch up and you wouldn't get a signal for a couple of hours, but of course sitting around in the marina it worked perfect. We showed it off to all who came aboard, and were the envy of the marina. One last important item before we left: Judy and Lee just had to have this little Chihuahua puppy she found in town. And so Pepper joined the crew.

We planned our shakedown run: down the west coast of Florida to Key West, then up to and across the Gulf Stream to Cat Island in the Bahamas; then from the Bahamas Bank, 150 miles across to Nassau.

The FBI was working hard to catch Les. At this point, they apparently didn't know about Judy, or at least much about her. Les's family—Joan and the kids, my mom and other relatives—were interrogated and telephones were bugged. Surveillance was not fun for his family members, and it only deepened Joan's distrust for Les as a father. It was extremely hard for his children to see their father on the front page of a newspaper. Les was not yet a "most-wanted criminal," but the Feds' interest was very high. Les was hot, so it was a good time to leave the country.

On our way to Key West, I thought we were doing well. The diesel was singing and it didn't matter what the weather was doing because we were leaving on another adventure. Then, only one month into our trip, we broke down.

Judy and Lee were trying to get some sleep, and it was about three a.m. and pretty rough seas. I had six-to-eight beers in me, so the rough water didn't matter much. Suddenly there was smoke—*What the fuck!* Then the engine stopped, so I ran down below and opened the engine room hatch. There was a lot of black smoke, but I didn't see any fire. After a very dirty exploration, it turned out we'd a broken exhaust pipe, and the engine room was a black carbon-coated mess. We couldn't use the motor, so we had to sail—that meant we had to head back to Florida. Damn!

After a lot of chat back and forth with the radio birds (has-beens, marinas, drunks, the bored, ex-boaters, etc.), a marina at Marathon talked us up the channel to their little backcountry yard and helped us tie up. The repair wasn't that difficult, but the exhaust made a huge mess. A couple of days later, we were back on our way to the Bahamas.

Once we got there, we quickly discovered we didn't enjoy Nassau very much, as it had way too many tourists and the prices were way too high. What we wanted was peace and quiet. The advice at the sailors' bar was to head for Highborne Cay, and follow the islands south. With our new Bahamas cruising guide chart open to the Exumas, we left.

Nassau, the capital of the Bahamas, is almost centrally located in the islands. From there you either go north or northeast to Eleuthera, the Abacos or the Grand Bahamas. These places were full of tourists and civilized. East and south, you're mainly on your own, so most cruisers went this way to make a loop through the islands around the tip of Cuba and down the Windward Passage to Jamaica, the Caymans, Mexico and back to Florida. Or you head to Puerto Rico from the Bahamas and the rest of the Caribbean, and normally those cruisers had kids. We headed east to

Les posing with a cardboard Reagan during his run.

a fuel stop in Highborne Cay, then down to what's called China Banks. No stores, but miles and miles of places to stop for a day or a couple of months.

The water was so clear, the bottom looked about six feet under the surface. Coral heads with black tops extending from the bottom looked very menacing—I knew they could knock a hole in a boat going ten knots like us. Although we had color charts telling us of the approximate depth of the water by the color—white or no color meaning you just ran aground! Dark blue meant have another beer!—I stationed Judy on the bow to direct us. I was yelling at everything that moved because I was in way over my head on this sailboat-across-the-world shit, and I took it out on Judy and Lee. That night, we were so tired we just anchored in the middle of a river, since traveling at night was sure suicide. Poor Judy must have nearly died of fright a hundred times that first day.

I don't know why I didn't think to rely on the depth gauge, outside of the fact it wasn't located right in front of the wheel; it was placed on the forward bulkhead of the cockpit with a plastic cover. We removed the plastic cover, and the gauge showed twelve- to eighteen-feet—but never lower than twelve-feet. So the pressure was lifted and Judy could relax. But it sure did look shallow!

We never did touch the bottom, and as we finally relaxed, we left the bank to cross the tongue of the ocean. It was a real deep channel that cut into the northern side of Paradise Island and Nassau. The water was so beautiful—a deep blue-purple. Sailing the boat into paradise had a lot more details to it than the dreams did, but it reminded us that life and dreams had a learning curve.

The next day, I had a hell of a time figuring out which way I was supposed to go. I could see a group of islands straight ahead—right where they were supposed to be on the chart—but I couldn't tell which one was my destination that had the deep water pass that we needed to take. The five thousand dollar satellite navigator was "searching" as we got closer, so it couldn't provide any answers. Things were getting confusing. It looked like we needed to be on the other side. Finally, Judy said, "Use the radio!" Why didn't I think of that? A quick call on the radio got us directions into the harbor. That's how it was in the Caribbean. We never got a bum direction, and the radio turned out to save our butts more than the satellite navigator. We still had to have one though! Crossing the ocean could be a bear without one. Of course, some years later we bought the next generation satellite navigator with G.P.S. It was one hundred percent better and very accurate down to three meters for $300!

After visiting Highborne and getting a tank of fuel, beer, and fresh fish we started the south odyssey of finding remote coves, seeing no one for days, endless swimming and discovering the bottom of the sea. We caught lobster and groper almost every day. We would see boats and wave, and then perhaps we

to be alone. We were anchored within about a 100' of each other, close enough to hear stuff at night on the water.

One night, our little dog, Pepper, gave us the sign that she had to take a dump. Now, I'd been on this dog's ass about where to "go" on the boat for most of the trip. Judy was always happy to clean it up, but I felt the dog had to learn where to go, period. By the time we got to the cove, Pepper had finally figured it out. I carried her up the ladder to the cockpit and onto the mat at the rear of the deck.

It was hot out, I'd had my beers and the Devil was coming out. I picked up the dog and carried her up to the cockpit. I looked over at our neighbor—who didn't even know we had a dog on board—and I thought I would stir things up a bit. There was no sign of the old man above deck, but there was a light on down below in his boat, so he was probably reading or something. So I slipped over the edge and down the swim ladder. I reached up and picked up the dog, who was wondering what in the hell was going on, and we swam very quietly over to the old man's boat. I placed the dog up on the transom of his boat, and quietly gave the dog the encouragement to go potty. "That's a good girl!" She performed well enough, and we swam back home like thieves in the night.

The next morning, I got up with the sun and went for my morning swim while watching for signs from my neighbor. Sure enough, he came out on deck and headed for the stern of his boat to take his morning pee. He looked down to see the little gift Pepper and I had left for him. At first, he had this I'm-really-not-awake look on his face. "What the hell kind of damn bird shits this big on my boat?!" he shouted. He kept looking around for the imaginary giant seagull. Then he kicked the mess overboard.

Over on *Tambourine Man*, we laughed ourselves sick.

That night, we were on someone else's boat, and I told the story to our friends. It was decided to have the "bird" re-visit our neighbor again so everyone could share the fun the next morning. Later, same story, I swam over to the boat and placed the dog on the deck, and she performed like a champ. Only this night she seemed to have had a larger than normal day of eating, and the result was a bit more rewarding!

Morning came with the whole camp up and waiting for the poor old guy to take his morning pee. Sure enough, he showed up right on time and began to take his morning relief. He looked down and the damn bird did it again! Bigger this time, but in the same place! He looked up to the sky and said, "What are the odds of a big bird twice in the same spot?" We were dying laughing! He complained to everyone who would listen, and nobody told him. He was constantly looking up at the sky. We never told our secret, and he left a few days later looking for a bird-free place in the sun.

Back before we left on our adventures, Judy and Lee took me—the Yankee—to my first Mardi Gras in New Orleans. I enjoyed the floats, the parade, the costumed groups that threw glass beads and replica coins into the crowd. Stuff was flying all over the place, covering the sidewalks and streets, as people and kids scooped up the souvenirs. Most of the aluminum coins were blue, amber, red, green and a lot of purple and gold. They have little value after Mardi Gras; ads appear in local papers buying the stuff back for next year, and the streets end up mostly clean.

As you can imagine, with a seven-year-old in tow, we ended up with a few pounds of the stuff. Later in the hotel, Lee saved the best of the best. We gave him a suitcase to hold his treasure. Lee's treasure found a berth in the 42' sailboat, even though space was at a premium. Lee was allowed his space, and he chose to take it.

A couple of weeks after the "Pepper caper," we found ourselves in a small lagoon with an entrance east to the sea. It was as beautiful as a dream: a crystal-white sandy bottom in the center and some sea grass at the entrance—a coral reef outside full of lobster and grouper. We dropped anchor and decided to stay for a while.

During a reorganization to find somewhere to put things, Lee's case of parade junk surfaced again. I realized that if I didn't talk Lee into surrendering his treasure, it was going to be with us for life! So one night, after many beers, the idea came to me to talk him into creating a treasure for all to enjoy. . .

Lee Wilson's first barracuda on *Mr. T.*

and rid our boat of the load. Lee could create a scene for kids after us. Lee immediately jumped on the idea. Over the next few days, we put bits of treasure throughout that lagoon with a few coins here, and a scattering of glass beads there. After a few days of tides and the sand shifting, and the scene was MGM quality. As the days passed, the picture would change. Some things disappeared, and others reappeared.

Every morning, Lee tended his garden and spent time marveling at his creation. As if in a script, a boat showed up one day with four kids, all swimmers ages eight to fourteen. We made our hellos and mentioned not a word of the treasure. Soon the anchoring duties were completed, the kids were swimming, and the adults were having cocktails and telling stories in our cockpit. Our new neighbors were explaining the trouble of boredom, four kids and small boats. Just at that moment, we heard a scream of "Look, look!" The two oldest had found two coins in the entrance of the grass, and they came screaming back in their dingy with their piece of the treasure. The coins were passed around that night many times, along with many theories, guesses and . . . our silence.

The next morning, Lee dove with his new friends and repossessed a few pieces of his own treasure—carefully giving nothing away. He even suggested a wild theory of his own to spice up the moment. By now the stuff was not that easily found, but they all ended up finding some and having great discussions about the possible value and who wanted to trade. Nobody seemed to notice that the coins were made of aluminum, and the nylon strings holding the glass beads together didn't fit the picture of pirate days either. But the boredom was gone.

The night before we left, with our secret intact, two other boats appeared and the hunt was on! As we pulled out, most were so busy combing the bottom we barely got a wave goodbye.

Months later, as we joined a few cruising boats in Jamaica looking for a hamburger and beer, we heard amazing stories of unbelievable amounts of treasures found south of Highborne Cay in the Exumas. Lee had the best story of them all—and a few coins to make it believable!

The early Eighties were the height of the cocaine drug-trafficking days, although Les had no interest in hard drugs. Since he was relatively new at sailing he decided that he would stay away from taking on any serious amounts of drugs on to the boat, even though it seemed a lot of fellow sailors were. He simply didn't know what to expect with the authorities to take that amount of risk. If he wasn't confident that he could pull off a job, then he would walk away. This was one of the main reasons that he eluded authorities for so long.

Toward the end of the Exumas and Crooked Cay, we crossed a bit of blue water and headed for the Great Inagua Island and

Matthew Town. Later that day, a white mountain appeared before us coming up out of the water. We all looked through the binoculars and couldn't figure out how white sand could be piled so high—the chart said nothing. As we got close, we could see black and yellow things moving about the top and sides. Finally, we got close enough that we could figure it out: it was a great salt mountain, owned by Morton Salt. Bulldozers were in constant motion, moving the salt around. We couldn't believe that there was that much salt in the entire world! We laughed our asses off at ourselves for not figuring it out earlier.

Matthew Town was the only real town on the island. There was no harbor—just a rock side to anchor on the lee side, and although it wasn't calm we were tired and slept well.

Lee woke us up the next morning telling us there was a big boat right outside calling for us. I stumbled up to the cockpit to find an old tramp freighter, a wooden 60' boat—a good little island trader—we'd met outside Cat Cay four or five months ago. They were having problems with their satellite navigation system, saw our antenna, and thought we might be able to help. We had the same model, but mine was much more complex. However, I was able to fix it by looking up the error messages in our manual.

We all stood and waved as the two guys were leaving. As they did, they threw us a coconut that had been neatly cut in two, stuffed full of pot and glued back together. It was a big coconut, too! I finally recalled that when we last met them, they had just returned from Jamaica to get a load of pot. They had black bags stacked everywhere down below stuffed to the brim!

Not much later, another boat came near that seemed to need our help. I yelled at them to shut it down and throw out the anchor, but they said they couldn't. They were having troubles with their prop that was a variable type without a transmission—you just change the pitch the way you want it, in forward or reverse, fast or slow. They yelled out, "It won't come out of pitch!" I understood they couldn't stop without shutting down the engine.

We convinced them to shut down and anchor, and we would get their prop fixed one way or another. Growing up in a family full of mechanical engineers I prided myself as being good at mechanical things. If I had the right tools I could fix it. That Mr. Fix-It attitude would come back to haunt me!

They made another long loop and came back ready to anchor and did it perfect. We took the dingy over and picked them up. Judy cooked up a great meal. They told us they needed water, food and booze. Because of the prop, they hadn't had a chance to get any groceries, only pot. Then they told us how they made it through the islands, across the Gulf Stream and landed in Florida without being captured. Youth!

The next day and the day after we worked on their boat and got it half right, so they at least could back it up and stop without killing the engine. The next morning they were gone. We really wished them good luck, not so much in breaking the law, but on their adventure. A year or so later, we found that they had success as we saw them in Key West.

During the trip, we picked up a hitchhiker in George Town who was also going to Jamaica and wanted to tag along. He only had a road map and a compass. His boat was never intended for off-shore work. So this 28' day-sailor with three people on board followed us like a baby duck. Immediately, tensions rose between us. The problem was speed. The little boat had a single cylinder nine horsepower diesel. With the sails up and the diesel running wide-open it could go six knots, tops. Our speed was eight to ten knots. As we drew away, the radio would crackle, "Don't leave us!" So without any alternative, we kept them in tow all day. The first night, I explained to the skipper how to "hove too." But one night, he came too close and some hours later, we bumped.

Bumping at sea is a very big no-no. The inertia of twelve tons coming together with five tons on a rolling ocean is the destruction of something. That night, Lee saved the day by fending the other boat away after the first bump with a push of the starter button. I was really mad since after all we had done for them they ran into us. I was already in the doghouse with Judy for helping them in the first place—she saw down the road clearer than I did.

The cap to the evening was when the Coast Guard called us on the radio. From their point of view on the radar screens at Guantanamo Bay, two boats coming together could be for only one reason—to pass something. I wasn't comfortable being thought of as a drug smuggler! It had no class. I talked my ass off to them explaining about the adopted boat and their fear of being left behind. It worked! Next stop would be Port Antonio, Jamaica.

Les was only interested in marijuana and beer. He didn't use hard drugs or even hard alcohol for that matter. At one point in Jamaica, where the beer was costing him two dollars a can, he decided he would give the rum a try. But that only lasted as long as the Jamaican trip and then it was back to beer. For Les, beer was one of the main food groups, and life without it wasn't worth living. Beer was his drug of choice—unlike the newspaper articles that falsely claimed Les to be a heroin addict and much more. When he calls me today, I make sure to tell him I'm having a beer, and that gets him every time.

We finally reached Port Antonio, after a few misunderstandings with the harbor police, around midnight, but everyone had gone home—welcome to Jamaica! But we did raise an old man on the radio who said he had a marina. He came right out in an inflatable and guided us in, and showed us where to anchor since

The *Viking* in Jamaica. 1984

there wasn't any room at the dock. The "marina" turned out to be a trawler with a broken-down dock and a six-stool bar.

The next morning, we got out the dingy and went in to check out the town after Customs got through with us. We found a nice open restaurant and were enjoying a hot breakfast when this kid came running up to our table saying, "Your boat is in the mangroves!" So I ran down to the dingy, and sure enough the anchor had dragged across the little bay and was in some weeds. There

101

wasn't any damage; it just messed up my breakfast. I re-anchored and went back to get Judy and Lee, and we walked the town that consisted mostly of bars and tourist shops with a lot of Rasta men. Within hours, everyone knew who belonged to what boat, and we were constantly provided with pot. They told us, "Say, when time comes to load up, come see me!" That happened every time we went to town.

After a week, we got a spot on some junk dock, but it did have water and power and a bar within twenty feet of the boat—heaven. Our little friends with the twenty-eight-footer took off for Montego Bay where he lived and was going to rent the boat to tourists. So we were free from them at last!

As boats came in, we developed a tight little group. There was the *W.C. Fields*, a restored 43' schooner with two couples; a 39' Ketch custom made in Norway of solid teak called *Viking* with a guy named Captain John sailing solo; an old three-masted brig full of students; a trawler owner and his Doberman pinchers that had about eaten up all the woodwork topside; and a crop-duster with a guy who knew everything about everything. We had great times partying and swapping stories.

All of us had to check our guns into the police for safe-keeping. We were told we'd get them back when we left. We wanted to see Montego Bay before we left, so we made arrangements to pick up the guns at the Montego Bay marina. We had two handguns and a Mini 14. We also kept a hand-grenade on board that was quite legal. A friend named Steve gave it to me and told me it was the ultimate weapon. When the pirates come alongside, you just lob it in their boat and duck. Problem solved. That sounded good to me, so I wrapped it up in a towel and put it in the bilge. I soon forgot about it—I didn't turn it in to the Jamaican police.

We took off with *W.C. Fields* and *Viking* a day behind. We enjoyed the town, but especially the real marina with all the bells and whistles with first class restaurants, bars and lots of nice boats that were mostly sports fisherman charter boats to go out in the channel for world-class fishing.

We picked up our guns alongside *W.C. Fields* and *Viking*. We thought that getting our guns back wouldn't be easy, but ours came in two days. *W.C. Field's* guns came also but missing one. Although we were technically cleared to leave, we waited one more day until they could get back their gun so we could travel together.

That afternoon, I was sitting in the cockpit having a beer, and a black man in a nice white shirt, black slacks, and a brief-case came down the dock and stopped at our boat. He asked, "How do you get on the boat?"

We were moored Mediterranean style, so it was a bit of a trick to get on board without falling in the drink. I answered him, "Carefully."

He asked, "May I come aboard?"

I explained to him, "Since Customs has cleared us to leave, we aren't allowed to have visitors." I thought, *Who is this guy?*

That was when he flashed his police badge. "I'd really like to talk to you." In Third World countries, with the police it's always about a bribe. I wondered what the scam was, but he talked me into welcoming him aboard.

As soon as he was aboard, he wanted to go down below. I was really getting a bit paranoid. He told me it was all right, but insisted we had to go down below to talk.

Once we were sitting around the table, he said, "I'd like to buy you and your lovely wife dinner. After which, I will leave you with this briefcase." He opened it up, and there was $75 thousand American dollars in it. When you get back to the U.S.A., just call this number." He handed me a business card. "A gentleman will offer to buy you dinner.

Judy asked, "When? Where in the States?"

He responded: "Anywhere in your homeland and whenever you like. Take your time—three to six months is perfectly fine."

I was dumbfounded, but it was Jamaica. It was well-known that if you wanted to be a successful smuggler, you dealt with the police. But I told him, "No way. We've been to all the wrong places. We'd never make it through Customs on our return. Filling up the boat with pot is stupid."

"Oh, no, it's not pot!" But he wouldn't say what it was his people would hide on the boat. "Don't worry. You'll never notice anything."

I knew every cranny on that boat—and I knew it wouldn't work. So I said, "No thanks." We knew if the Coast Guard caught you with drugs, they had a no-tolerance policy. You could lose your half-million dollar boat with no arrest—they'd just put you on the beach, take the boat, and be gone. Of course, you could take the American way by fighting it in the courts, but by the time you got to court and the judge said you could have your boat back, it'll have been at least a year. Then there'd be no boat left and everything would be gone but the attorney fees. At that time, 250 pounds of pot in Miami was worth $250 thousand— more if you took it up north to Boston or New York, as one of our friends did. That was a lot of money for smuggling pot that everyone involved considered an easy "victim-less crime." It was our first trip around the Caribbean, and we didn't want to take the gamble.

He was real nice about it, thanked us for our time and wished us luck. As he was walking away, he waived at another boat. I knew that boat was "loaded" because they were friends and told us, plus they weren't going to stop at the Caymans or Mexico. We were one of the only boats that wasn't loaded up.

All three boats sailed together from Jamaica. It was ideal sailing—almost entirely downwind, which I actually don't prefer. We sailed side by side for hours. *W.C. Fields* was worried about having any loose pot on board, so at cocktail time we would come alongside and throw them a night's worth.

We had a system of keeping all the personal-use drugs in one place—a tackle box with holes drilled in it with a heavy steel bar. When you saw the Coast Guard coming you had to be ready since, as I mentioned, they had a no-tolerance policy.

The morning of the third day we were in the Caymans and bid our friends lots of luck and farewell.

The Caymans were beautiful. We anchored right off George-town's Seven-Mile Beach in front of all the fine hotels. They didn't really mind. The sight of sailboats anchored off their hotels did nothing but add charm, so some even welcomed us with free showers and beach rights. Of course, we ate there and at least went to the bar, so it worked out good.

Upon anchoring you raise the Q flag for customs and im-migration to come check you in. No passports were needed, just a driver's license. They were very professional. The boat also had to be fumigated, so they came on board with these shiny tanks that were really space ship-style stuff. We had a little discussion of how the fumes might just kill our little three-pound Pepper, so they gave us a good checking for plants and fruit and let us go without spraying.

After we were done, we moved back to the beach and an-chored beside a couple other boats and turned in for the night. We had a deal with Lee that he was never to wake us up short of being run down by a tanker, but the next morning he couldn't keep to himself. He came in yelling, "Mom! Mom! Mom! You gotta see this!"

So I went up to the cockpit and looked where Lee was point-ing. There was a Burger King that was about 200 feet away! It'd been a year or so since we had hamburger and fries. I raced down to dress and get Judy up. Then we hopped into the dingy and headed for the Burger King.

I think we each tried to eat one of everything. Then I noticed the prices. Damn! We'd spent about $28—a lot more than at home! It took me a while to figure out the exchange rate was about $1 to about 80 cents Cayman, but it still seemed pretty high for a burger meal.

After we finished eating, we walked downtown—which wasn't very big. However, it did have something like thirty-eight banks with names like Jones and Brown. I was certainly interested in them! With only about twenty miles of roads on the entire island you'd be amazed at how many Corvettes there were in town!

We returned to the dingy—and saw our sailboat going out to sea backwards! The anchoring was in pure white sand with beautiful coral patches, and our anchor had dragged all the way to where the sea bank drops off to deep, deep water. So the boat was drifting with the anchor straight down, touching nothing. In our rush to get to Burger King, we hadn't put the motor on the dingy. I told Judy to stay and call someone if she saw that I wasn't going to catch the boat. I went off, rowing like a madman. At first, it didn't look like I was gaining, but I then noticed an inflatable going alongside our boat, then someone jumping aboard. I had my back to the boat, and I was concentrating on rowing smoothly. When I did turn again I noticed the boat was coming my way. I noticed a guy at the helm who definitely knew what he was doing. He had the diesel going and the anchor chain was hanging down, so I tied up the dingy and thanked him for saving my boat. I asked him how he knew how to start the engine, and he told me proudly he could drive anything. Bob and I became good friends after that.

He'd been in the boat anchored next to us, and when he noticed me rowing hard and our boat going out to sea, he hopped in his dingy and saved my fucking day. He helped me re-anchor, and we could see in the super clear water where my anchor had marched around about four coral heads leaving a four foot trench right out to sea. It was pretty impressive.

Bob flew for American Airlines. He'd come from Miami with his new boat and wife for some reason. His wife ended up going home. He was an avid diver and stuck it out without a diving buddy, but he was in a funk. We went in and picked up Lee and Judy and came back to the boat for a nice afternoon of cocktails and conversation. The guy right away wanted to know if I was a diver. "Sure, a little," I said. He meant scuba and I meant snorkeling—anyway, I had no gear. No problem, he had tanks, fins, masks and the works.

"Tomorrow morning, OK?" He was a very thorough teacher, and I wasn't the least bit hesitant about diving. I had just never experienced it before. Bob went every day to get the bottles filled, and we dove and dove in some of the prettiest water and around the most interesting wrecks I'd ever seen.

One day, Bob told me he'd run out of time, and he had to get back to Miami for work. Work is indeed the curse of the drinking

Les rigging on *Mr. T* before leaving the Bahamas.

class! He was a little concerned about sailing back to Miami by himself. He asked me to go and he would fly me back. I couldn't leave Lee and Judy like that, and I assured him that sailing solo was actually a great time and he'd enjoy the accomplishment.

I got his number, Judy cooked one last good meal and then he was gone. We never saw him again, but he did leave me with a complete set of diving equipment.

Busted

*L*es only had the equivalent of a high school education, but he was extremely bright, loved to learn new things, and could do almost anything, especially mechanically. While he was in prison, he was given an I.Q. test. He came out at genius status. That didn't come as a big surprise to some. Some people are extremely intelligent; they simply don't channel their smarts in the best direction. One could say Les was too smart for his own good. Judy was a good companion for him, since she was very level-headed and kept him focused.

We decided to head to Cancún—another 400 miles downwind. Once we neared the Yucatan Peninsula, we aimed for La Isla Bay on the west side of La Isla Mujeres. Back in 1983, not a whole lot of tourists had found Isla Mujeres as they had Cancún across the bay. It was a little piece of heaven.

The Mexican Navy had a post there and a military airport. It had a shrimp dock and modern hotel. The north end had been torn up in a hurricane. Only the hippies were living in some deserted hotel rooms, otherwise, no one was there. There was a coral reef right in the bay, El Garrafón Marine Park at the south end of the island. They had motor scooters for rent there. And everything was dirt cheap.

Les and Judy in a little boat in Isla Mujeres, Mexico.

It was a very, very nice place, so we decided to stay awhile. Our visas were good for six months, so we stayed eight. The immigration guy ended up being our pot connection. He had kids in school to pay for, so he told us.

It was so much fun that we started learning Spanish. The native people were so kind in correcting our miserable tries, but we stumbled along fine after a while. They seemed to appreciate our attempts.

My first Spanish lesson came at one of our first Mexican restaurant experiences. We picked a nice-looking restaurant that was a bit off the tourist trail. Looking at the menu was worthless, although Judy found the word *pollo*. We knew that meant chicken, and that was what she wanted. I saw the word *salsa*— and I knew what that meant. I also saw the word *verde*, and I was pretty sure that was green—so that meant green salad, right? When we ordered, the waitress asked if that was all. I could tell by her look that she had some questions for me, but we couldn't communicate. Oh, and beer—*cerveza*. I knew that one.

Busted

Judy's chicken came real nice, but I got a bowl that wasn't salad. I decided it must be soup, even though it was cold. It came with a big spoon, that wasn't really a soup spoon, I noticed two heads peeking out of the kitchen door and the waitress was also looking our way. I wondered what they wanted. I took a big spoonful—and almost lost consciousness and shit myself at the same time! *Salsa Verde* was *hot*—not just hot, but *motherf'ucking* hot! Everyone was laughing, and I literally couldn't breathe. The waitress came over to me with a big glass of water that didn't come close to helping. I downed the beer and signaled for another. Judy was laughing so hard she couldn't breathe. It was funny, I have to admit.

We had many adventures in Mexico. During one bus trip, we bought a baby spider monkey in Merida. We got a ride back with five people and our suitcases in a V.W. bug. Ola was the center of attention most of the time. The pronunciation of her name in Spanish means hello, and old Mexico is a very polite place where everyone seemed to say *hola* on the sidewalk. So Ola thought everyone knew her.

Ola, Les and Judy's spider monkey, inside *Mr. T.* in Mexico.

She was incredibly smart. She could get out of anything if you locked her in. We didn't even try to tie or hide anything because it would be gone. I smoked Lucky Strikes at the time, and she would copy Dad and put them in her mouth, then go find the lighter. If she could have made the lighter work with a thumb she would have.

One day, I decided to make a nice cage for Ola with some cabinet materials and even a couple dowels. We needed the cage because we couldn't leave without Ola. My main fear was having her go up in the rigging where the top of the mast was 57' tall, but she played over the boat like a jungle gym and never showed any interest in going up high. I guess we could have locked her inside on the boat, but Judy wouldn't think of it. She would say, "My little girl can just go with." We made a day of it, taking the ferry and a cab to get into the "big city" of Cancún. It was hard to find a lumber yard, and even harder to communicate all I wanted. But finally we got all that accomplished and went back to the boat.

I spent the entire next day designing, drilling and leveling. I even managed to get a swing in there! Then the moment of truth came as we showed Ola her new home.

Only she wasn't going to have anything to do with it. Nope.

I threw a banana into the cage, hoping she would follow such a treat. She loved them, but we didn't give them to her often. We kept her on a dry dog food diet to keep the poop firm, so a banana was a big treat. She went for it and I slammed the door shut. She looked around, then looked at us, then looked around again. Calmly, she ate the banana. Then she went over to the gate and ripped the dowels out like they were noodles. So much for cage life. We never tried to lock her up again.

After one long cocktail hour, we thought that being on a boat, you needed to know how to swim—it was required. Pepper could swim, although she didn't like it and couldn't swim far, but she could do it. So it was swim lessons for Ola.

Busted

The water was about eighty-five degrees and very nice—perfect for learning how to swim. I was in the water at the foot of the boarding ladder, and Judy was sitting on the deck with her feet hanging over the ladder. Ola knew something was going on, so she held on real tight to Mama. I coaxed her in and held out my arms for her to come to me, and finally she did. She didn't know anything about the water though. I splashed her, and she splashed me back. I held her out and lowered her in, then let go. Ola looked at me with wide-open eyes, full of fright—that told me she'd never trust me again. She didn't make one little movement to swim as she sank with her little arms stretched out toward me.

Apparently spider monkeys do not swim.

I reached down, pulled her up and close. She spat out the salty water, clearly mad. I was in the dog house for three days before she would come to me again.

We fell in love with that monkey. At one point there was a doctor captaining a boat in the harbor and Judy asked him if he would give us a birth certificate for Ola so we could bring her back through Customs. I remember her explaining how it would work: if Customs made a fuss about the primate, she would whip out the birth record and get real indignant about him berating her daughter! We really enjoyed that idea!

We had stayed so long that our friend Thomas at the immigration office—which got almost zero business except for the gringo boats—knew us by sight. We were coming to the end of our six month visa. But he said, "Don't worry. If you want to stay longer, I can extend it one time if you leave for at least twenty-four hours." We appreciated his help, as we were really into taking it easy.

One morning, we noticed a fishing boat coming up to our boat with Thomas and some local cops, with one guy who looked like the boss. We put out our fenders, and before I knew it our cockpit was full of officials.

Thomas told me, "The *comandante* is here to buy your machine gun and wants to see it."

In Mexico, you're allowed to keep your firearms aboard—just don't bring them to land. The Mini-14 caliber machine gun that we had was mounted in spring clips above the ladder going out to the cockpit, and everyone had seen it that had been on board. It was a sharp-looking stainless steel gun, which, when I was in Albuquerque, I'd taken to a Harley bike shop to have it polished. The stock was flat black, the clips were chrome plated. The officers who checked us in had seen it, and obviously word had gotten to the *comandante*, who was sort of the chief of police.

We were getting short of money, and I didn't really need the gun, I'd just never thought of selling it before. Selling weapons in Mexico was a real bad crime, and here came this *comandante* who wanted to buy it! I really had no choice, given who he was.

Thomas whispered to me that the *comandante* was a very macho man. Cinco de Mayo was coming up, and he wanted to ride up front at the parade waving that pretty gun.

I handed it to him, and his eyes went wide.

Through Thomas, he said, "Oh, this is beautiful! How much?"

"$350," I told him.

"How many bullets?" he asked.

All I had was two clips that held forty bullets, which I showed him.

Rattling off something to Thomas, he climbed back into the fishing boat—with my gun!

I asked Thomas what was going on. "Oh, he says to come by his office for the money."

Judy and I watched them leave. I said to her, "I've never been ripped off so smoothly before! Who the hell wants to go to the police station?"

We did end up going to the police station. It took three trips, as the *comandante* paid us in installments—I got a brown bag of pesos each time. He was very nice, and we got to know all the cops. Pretty amazing for a bank thief to have cop friends!

Sometime later, Thomas came to the boat again. He told me, "Please bring your wife and papers to the immigration office to-morrow morning."

I asked him, "What's this all about?"

"Some *jefe* from El Distrito Federal is here to see you."

"OK, see you tomorrow," I said.

It couldn't be good news. El Distrito Federal meant Mexico City was somehow involved. We spent the night wondering and worrying. We could've just pulled up and left, but the Navy was right there. Plus we simply didn't know what was going on. What could it be? We'd done nothing that the Mexican immigration would want to talk to us about.

The next day, we went to the office. Thomas was there with his wife. "Please, sit down," he said, indicating the table set as if for guests. "Do you want anything to drink?"

I noticed a man standing in the back corner looking at a piece of paper.

He walked over and introduced himself as being there at the request of the FBI. He showed me a letter from the FBI that was four months old. It wanted the authorities to check and see if Les Rogge was on the *Tambourine Man* anchored in La Isla Bay, Cancún. There was a photo.

That was my name on the letter. And the name of the boat was correct. But the photo wasn't me! Someone really screwed up. It was obvious we were going to get through this one all right.

The man gave us his apologies, then said, "We should take your photo and fingerprints for the record so you don't have any problems in the future."

Shit! This isn't good! I needed time to think about it, but to refuse wouldn't be much better. Then the man discovered that the camera didn't have any film! I said, "You know, I think my fingerprints will be enough for the FBI to figure all this out."

Thomas whipped out his ink pad, and I tried my best to smudge the prints. I think I did a good job.

We left there bewildered as to how the FBI knew where we were. Who knew my real name? I hadn't used it with the boat broker—or anyone in recent memory. Judy and her folks knew me as Don Rose. They'd never heard my real name. All we knew for sure was, we thanked God that the Mexican government was so slow!

Judy called Grandma to ask if the FBI had come snooping around, or if there'd been anything about me on the news. But Grandma knew nothing.

Just to be safe, we decided to send Lee back with Grandma. We'd been thinking about sending him home for some time, since he wasn't having a good time. There was a language problem for him, and there just weren't any kids for him to play with. Back home, he would have lots of stories to share with his friends. Reluctantly, we put him on a plane to Houston where Grandma and Floyd would pick him up.

After the inquiry, we were wondering if we had to dump the boat. Instead, we decided to get the hell out of there. But when we sat down to plot out the short hop to Key West that was 350 miles along the Gulf Stream, the satellite navigation was dead. I had to call Texas Instruments in Dallas—which meant I had to check into one of the high rise hotels with international phones—*three times*. Finally, Texas Instruments offered to send us a new one. I arranged with Thomas—because he worked at the airport two days a week—to duck the thirty percent import tax.

Everything went wrong though. I went in to get the package at the Customs chief's office. It was sitting on the floor of his office. He just kicked it toward me. I thought that was it, and we walked out with the box to the parking lot and took off in our friend's V.W. We didn't get far, though, as the feds pulled us over with drawn guns not far from the airport. We were brought back and charged with sneaking electronics into the country. I found an airline pilot in the airport who would translate for us. We stayed out of jail, but left without the navigator. We got an import/export agency to help us get the machine, and the lady was able to straighten it out, but it had to stay in bond for seventy-two hours. By then, our visas would be really expired, but we had no other choice—and I was pretty sure Thomas would look the other way.

We knew Ola couldn't come, because American Customs would never allow the importation of a monkey. So we had to find a foster home for her. Thomas helped out by finding an agent from Acapulco who had kids and a male spider monkey who would give Ola a good home. It was a real tear-jerker as she knew we were giving her away, and at one point she jumped back into my arms as we were leaving.

I went to the Navy base to get a weather fax since a hurricane had just blown by to the east about two days earlier. I wanted to make sure it was well north and hadn't doubled back—and wasn't out there looming for us. The Navy base gave me a weather report, but it was for a plane! I finally got to take a look at sea level, and it was a bit rough but winding down. Heading north looked good.

As soon as the new satellite navigation was hooked up, we said our goodbyes and headed out of Cancún Bay on the north side with strong gusty winds from the SSE to push us toward Key

West. Our friend John Smith from Grenada and his home-built boat went with us. He had a bad leak and needed to haul out in Miami.

The seas were huge, and with the wind blowing 20-30 knots *Tambourine Man* was flying. *Mr. T* was a very strong boat with extra strong rigging, and when we bought our cruising main sail it had battens to reef it down because we had a dogger boom. It would roll the claws out of the main track coming down, and that was OK, but going back up was a real pain in the ass. Trying to raise the main and feed the claws in the tracks at the same time required two people, and there was only the two of us, so who would steer?

When the wind got strong, we heeled more and went faster and never had a problem. We had our main up in a 40 knot wind before we would bring the whole sail down. Traditional old sailors would say we were crazy, but what did they know?

John was somewhere behind us in the dark. His complete list of electronic equipment included a VHF radio and a car battery. He didn't have any lights. It was a nice, fast, very long and wide boat with a shallow draft—and a stolen telephone pole for a mast. It sailed right along with us for most of the time, and faster in some points in the wind.

Early one morning, I went to the back to take a leak, and as I was hanging onto the backstays (we had two) I realized the tension was like a banjo string—really, really tight. I couldn't remember ever having that much strain on them before. The boat was surfing at times. On the back side we reached 13 knots before plowing into the next wave. Just then, I heard Judy yelling up at me, "Slow this fucker down!" The stick was pumping as our mast was bending in the middle as gusts hit it coming up off of the waves and catching a shot of clean air. So I rolled in the head sail—probably just in time to ward off a disaster, and we slowed way down. All was good again. My drunk-ass was having a ball—this was sailing!

Then all of a sudden, two large spotlights lit up the cockpit like lightening! I heard the crack of the radio: "This is the United States Coast Guard. State your citizenship, port of call, destination, how many on board, type of firearms," blah, blah, blah.

I got short with them saying it was really rough out and I couldn't talk and drive safely. The radio went silent. Then I heard John. Him I answered. He was obviously drunk because he told me when he gave the word to turn to port because I had pirates on my stern and he would give them hell with his "50"! The Coast Guard had gotten between us, but they couldn't see him on their radar because of his all-wooden boat. They turned their lights off us to search for the boat with the big gun.

We came off the wind and turned sharply to a port tack going due west. I could hear John giving them shit on the radio. He'd finally figured out it was the U.S. Coast Guard, and not pirates, that were the source of the lights and grumpy radio calls and had decided to have a little fun with them. He flaunted his Grenadian citizenship—which meant the Coast Guard had to radio to get permission from Grenada to board his boat—which would take hours, at least. That was how we left John and the Coast Guard—and I was sure I knew who would win that battle. Soon we couldn't see John anymore at all.

It was November of 1983, and the heat was getting even worse. The FBI had been building their case and now knew all about Judy. Judy's family members were aggressively interrogated. If the FBI thought you were in any way connected to Les or Judy, they would use you for information, and cause trouble for all involved. There would be legal fees for those who were interrogated to get their lives back. In one case, an acquaintance's life would never be the same. But for the most part, the people who came into Les's life and found out what he did for a living, would go to bat for Les and not turn him in even though there was always reward money available. That's how sincere their relationships were, and often they kept in touch with their favorites. There are many drawbacks to a life on the road of running, but they appreciated a quiet life of friends and family and getting to know people along the way.

When we got back to Key West, we called Customs as we were supposed to—even though we didn't know if they were looking for us or not. They told us they were busy and gave us clearance over the phone. Obviously they weren't even bothering to check the FBI alerts. It seemed that the government's left hand didn't know what its right hand was doing! Judy was so mad. She wanted me to call back and insist that they come down to the boat! We could have brought Ola back with us.

Life back in the States was a bit of a shocker: fast food, English, anything you needed was readily available. We re-entered the fast lane pretty quickly.

We stayed at a marina where we only paid eight dollars per foot, that included cable, phone, water and power, and life was good.

Judy and I got in the habit of getting high at night and walking up the road to a very, very nice restaurant for some key lime pie and coffee—since there was no way we could afford the meals on my salary. Sometimes we would have a bottle of wine there and leave feeling mighty fine. Every night we would pass this 50' black-hulled Coast Guard boat that never seemed to move. We would stop to look it over, and I came to covet their stainless steel anchor chain. I had always wanted a stainless steel anchor and chain since after a year or so a normal steel chain would rust and make a nasty mess as you pulled them up. The drawback was that stainless chain was about ten dollars a pound, so it was a wish only. The Coast Guards' rig was a real nice CQR (a popular plow anchor) that weighed about eighty-five pounds—a bit heavy for *Mr. T*, but you can't have too much ground tackle. It had a three-eighths inch chain, which was the right size for my winch. So every night, as we walked by that boat, I plotted how to get that chain. After about a week I had my plan. I would tie a long piece of "little stuff"—braided quarter-inch nylon that was used around a boat to tie up most everything and very strong—to my boat. The other end of the nylon rope I'd tie to the anchor, drop it and the chain in the drink, and pull it up to my boat into the chain locker.

I went aboard the Coast Guard boat to tie up the anchor, and things were going just fine. But as I tried to lift some chain up out of the hole in the deck—*clang! clang! clang!* It seemed like the loudest noise I'd ever heard. Then it dawned on me the deck was all aluminum, and that chain going through the aluminum pipe made such a racket that no one in their right mind would steal that chain! I aborted my mission—but I still remember that chain and how good it would have looked on our boat.

A couple of months after arriving at Stock Island Marina, it was rumored that the owner of the Houston Oilers had bought the place. I didn't ever find out who bought it, but the next month the rent almost tripled and went up to $1,100 a month. So we pulled out and anchored across from a nice restaurant close to where Judy got a waitressing job. I would row her into work in our dingy and row back to pick her up. A couple of times, it rained and her black uniform got soaked. I felt so sorry for her, but we needed the cash. She never complained.

After a month or so, a spot opened up on the bank next to the restaurant, and the slip had power. Around this time, Judy got a call from home saying that her parents had been interrogated by the FBI. Grandma asked her to return. Judy said she would be there right away. We knew then that the left hand had found the right hand!

That night, we left for Boot Cay and anchored out. I went over the stern and gave our baby a new name—the boat became *Expression*. I felt sure if the FBI was at Grandma's house looking for Judy, then they were closing in on us.

The next day, we headed for Tavernier and a little funky marina where our friend Steve docked his boat. It was a quiet little place with canals carved out and lined with limestone sometime after the Second World War. You certainly couldn't afford to cut those canals today. On the other side was a little airport that was simply a landing strip that served as a breakwater on the north shore. The marina had a cut that had a travel lift and a small dock that held less than a dozen boats—for us it was the perfect hiding place. We already knew half the people there, and they didn't ask questions.

I borrowed a car and got Judy on a flight to Lake Charles. She took Pepper with her, since the dog just adored her and would have been mopey without Mama. We worked out a plan to talk on the phone.

I worked my magic on a photocopier and came up with a new set of I.D. for myself. Then I went up to Miami, took the driver's test and came out with a new Florida driver's license in the name of Mr. Nelson.

At one point, Les went with a boatload of people on a diving trip off the coast of a South American country, known for their illegal imports to the States. The group was diving in shallow waters when they came across some stainless steel, old-fashioned milk jugs that were tied together with a large stainless steel chain. The team went back to the boats, gathered all the cutting equipment they had, and headed back to the spot to see if they could free one of the jugs. They used every tool they had, and finally opened one. It was completely filled with wet money. They took it back to the boats, split the cash and tried to decide what to do next. Les had wet money stuck to the inside of the cabin. Knowing when to say when was one of Les's skills that kept him on the run for over a decade, so when his new friends went back for more, Les split. He waited for his friends at a nearby port for several months, but they never returned. Les knew it was drug money and assumes someone had been watching the area. He figures his friends got in trouble when they went back. That money funded his life for the next several months, but eventually it ran dry, too.

Judy's calls were not good news. The FBI was all over her wanting to know everything and anything. I was sitting all right at the moment, but I'd pulled the boat to have the bottom painted, and the bill was now due. I was about broke, too.

Steve, who lived on a cabin cruiser—a boat that would never see the ocean again—was broke as well. He and I were sitting in the cockpit one evening looking out at a small landing strip beside the marina. A small twin engine plane landed, and a U-Haul truck came alongside to unload something. It was getting too dark to see many of the details, but it seemed like some sort of opportunity that we had to check into.

The next night, we had a burger at the food stand down the road and learned that the strip was leased by the D.E.A.—those planes were bringing in confiscated dope! The U-Haul trucks were transporting the goods somewhere. We decided to steal back the evidence. Obviously that U-Haul was taking the pot to some sort of storage facility.

After a few days of patiently watching, Steve, his girlfriend, Sally, and I managed to follow the U-Haul north up to Coral Springs. At a big interchange, the truck turned into the shadows where there was a massive mini-warehouse complex. We followed the truck right to the garage they intended to leave the dope in. It wasn't a normal storage unit, though. The facility had a phony wooden office in the front; they unloaded bails of pot into a back area. We were all excited because there was no security that we could see. The D.E.A. office had some strange-looking antennas on the roof—probably the alarm system had a radio frequency that would notify someone of a break-in.

When the U-Haul left, we went up to the front gate to inspect the construction. It was a heavy roll-up door with two locks and a latch in the cement floor. They didn't want anybody in there. It was obvious we were going to have to do a smash and dash job. But a bale that size was $10 thousand cash all day long. Two or three of those babies would get us out of debt.

We needed something heavy to deal with that front roll-up door, and Steve's van wasn't going to hack it. On the perimeter road of the warehouse complex were parked vehicles of all sorts that included R.V.s, trailers, trucks and boats. We found an old Mack truck cab with a huge front bumper with a lot of weight. We got it hotwired without too much trouble, but the battery was very dead. The battery was outside under the cab step, and it was huge. But there were jumper cables in the cab. We hadn't come equipped to do all of that work, but the beers said, "Go ahead!"

After swiping some batteries off the tongue of an Air Stream trailer, the Mack barked to life with a huge cloud of black smoke. I drove up to the storage door and discovered the truck wouldn't turn sharply enough to aim directly at the door, so I had to go back and forth to aim straight.

Wham! The truck knocked down the door with no problem, but our drunken asses didn't think that the truck was too high! The door became wedged under the opening, trapping the truck halfway in, right at the cab doors. In the slight panic of back and forth, the truck came out along with the door that fell on half of the phony office front and deck. We had to climb over the thing to go to the back where all the bales were stacked. The job was getting totally unbelievable, but still nobody seemed to take any notice.

We got our three bales in the van and got the hell out of there. Once we were up on the freeway, it was all high-fives. It was a relief that the worst burglary on record was over.

We stopped for a six-pack, and it took a few miles for our hearts to calm down. We had about $30 thousand worth of pot in the back and felt pretty good about that.

Sally started to inspect the haul. She asked, "Why do the bales have a red X on them?"

"Inventory marks," I told her.

"Why do they smell so funny?" she asked.

Steve whispered, "Girls! What do they know, right?"

Finally, we pulled up next to Steve's boat, and unloaded our treasure. Sally was right, there were spray-painted red Xs on the black plastic wrapping—and they *did* smell funny. We decided to smoke some as the final OK for our efforts. As we opened up the plastic, there was a strong odor of something—and it wasn't marijuana! We still smoked it—or at least a couple of tokes. Then it dawned on us that the reason for the lack of security at the mini-warehouse was because the stuff was worthless. It had been spiked with diesel fuel! But you could still go to jail for it.

It had been a long day that ended with throwing the bales back in the ocean down the road at the overpass. We were then back at square one with my boat on the hard with an $800 bill for the bottom paint job and almost flat broke.

A couple of nights later, I was sitting at a bar trying to find a path out of my money woes, when I heard these guys at a table talking about bank robbery—one of my main interests. One guy said, "There's never been a bank robbery near Key West because there's only one long road over a hundred miles long out there with no way to get away."

Up till now, I really hadn't given banks much thought. A quick job would get me out of debt. The hell with the long road—I had a boat! I was in bank robbery mode again, one hundred percent.

I had to get my sailboat in the water. But the marina owner had put a lien on my boat for the money I owed him for the hull painting. I didn't blame him. He had very little room for anything, and had a bunch of boats that were finished but unpaid. I laid a story on him that if he would give me a week to ten days, I'd pay my bill and get in the water. I didn't need the sailboat to rob the bank, but it would provide the final getaway to the Bahamas to wait for Judy. So back to work I went.

It didn't take long to find a bank with an all-female crew of six people. It was on Islamorada, down toward Key West, about ten miles from the boatyard.

Next: a getaway car. Steve ran me up to Homestead, where a Toyota dealer kept the demo keys in little boxes on the windows. There was no chain or fence to deal with. On this excursion, I had my tools with me, which included a pair of aviation metal cutters. I cut open the box with a hacksaw, and then I had the keys to a year-old white Toyota with plates. We had hand-held radios from the boat so we could talk if there was a problem, but there were none. I drove a few miles, then pulled over to change to the plates that I swiped a couple of days earlier from another dealer.

Two miles north of the bank was a condo with under-building parking that was never crowded. That's where I parked the Toyota. There was a path to a dock that had a few boats in slips—and the end of the dock was free. It was very low-key and no one would notice the car or me walking in and out.

Sally offered to dye my silver hair with a brown tint that would wash out in the shower or with a swim. I talked a young couple who lived in the marina into lending me their inboard speedboat in exchange for replacing a prop they'd bent.

Eight days later, on June 4th, I was ready to go. I spent my last few dollars picking up my suit at the cleaners. Steve took me to the Toyota. I had the radio to talk to him, my scanner, a shoulder holster and an attaché case with a folding jump bag inside. My hair looked great. Steve and Sally were both amazed that I would do something like rob a bank.

The manager of the bank was a female, probably around forty or so. I had made an appointment over the phone to talk to the manager about changing banks, which they always liked. I got into her office before I showed her the note to read. I opened my coat just enough for her to see the butt of the gun in the shoulder holster, and then I set the scanner on her desk and adjusted the squelch as I told her that it monitored her alarm system. If it went off I would shoot her and walk out. That amount of talk was usually enough to get all the cooperation I needed to be successful.

That lady had a bit of spark to her. I could tell that the robbery was pissing her off as she stared at me aggressively. I'm sure she thought I had no chance of escaping. I told the vault clerk to follow my written instructions or her boss would be shot—let's not turn this into a homicide! Just a bluff of course, but I said it with a steady stare that conveyed sincerity. I waited at her desk facing the manager, staring directly at her, as the clerk went to the vault to fill the bag. The clerk came back with my bag. It wasn't full, but I wasn't going to complain. I knew the robbery would never be solved, so it was free money and more than I needed, but not more than I wanted.

I had this little key from a Mercedes that had a red and green diode on it that lit up if you pushed the handle a certain way. I explained that if the vault clerk put anything other than paper in the bag—a dye pack or beeper for instance—the light would turn red, and I would shoot the manager. It was obviously another bluff, but I hated getting dye packs. Most banks didn't keep dye packs or other types of anti-theft stuff in the vaults because of accidents. It was very unlikely that there was anything other than money in that bag.

I zipped the bag, told them, "Thank you for your cooperation," picked up the scanner from her desk and headed nice and
slow for the front door. The white Toyota sedan was parked so
everyone could see it. I wanted them to tell the police. I hopped
in and drove around the block.

I parked under the condo and looked around. I saw nobody.
I took off my suit and put the money and everything in a big
cooler that I had in the back seat. I had shorts, and a t-shirt on
underneath the suit. Now I looked like an ordinary guy going
boating as I carried the cooler out of the garage and down to
the dock. Steve and Sally had the motorboat ready. As I stepped
aboard, we were off. After ten minutes, we were safely offshore.
Steve stopped the boat. I jumped in the water with soap and
washed the dark brown out of my hair.

Sally asked, "How much money did you get?"

"I have no idea. I didn't look." Steve looked like he would
bust, so I said, "Go ahead and count it."

After a quick tally, it came to $40 thousand "Perfect," I said,
climbing back in the boat. "We don't have to worry about money
for a while."

We opened some beers and sat and listened to the scanner.
"Last seen heading north in a white Toyota, plate number so and
so. . . ." A road block was up at the bridge where US1 goes over
the Intracoastal Waterway. All was well. We took the boat back
to the marina and partied on Steve's boat into the night.

The next morning, I sent the guy who owned the speedboat
to the marina manager to tell him that he was going to charter
my boat, and was going to pay for the yard bill. Please set the
boat into the water. I was staying away from the marina manager
because even with my hat my hair was darker than it was. I didn't
want to bleach it right then. I wanted to leave.

Sally kept reminding me that the description of the robber
was five-foot-seven, dark Latino with curly black hair, age about

forty. So much for eyewitness reliability. I still wanted to move on. I had my new set of I.D. So now the boat had a new name, and so did I.

I called Judy, and she said Floyd wasn't doing very well. I told her I was going to Staniel Cay where there was a little airfield to wait for her.

I decided to take Steve and Sally to the Bahamas with me for the company. Steve had to return the rental car to Miami. So he drove and Sally and I sailed the boat up to Miami to meet him at a marina. All we needed to start the cruise were groceries; a call to the local public market that sold yacht packages took care of that. We gave them the number of people and the number of days, and they would fix you up in grand style—everything from peanuts to caviar, if that was your taste. We took the steak/hamburger range with some wine, olives and cheeses. They delivered real fast, too. It was expensive, but we made up for it by calling the local beer distributor who gave us a deal on thirty-five cases of Stroh's Beer delivered to the boat. By sundown the boat was sitting real low with barely room for us!

We got out of there early, and by late afternoon we were docked and checked into Cat Cay Marina. It was private and expensive, but they would check you into the Bahamas real easy without questions or searches.

We took our time and worked our way down the Exumas to Staniel Cay to wait for Judy to arrive. I called Grandma's to talk with Judy. She was all upset. The FBI had been there looking for me. They seemed surprised to find her there without me—and were just sure I was somewhere nearby. She knew that the phones were tapped. Even though the boat and our names were no longer what the Feds were looking for, it wouldn't take them long to figure things out.

I told Judy to hang in there, and I would think of something. For sure that phone was no good, so moving was the most urgent thing to do right then. For some reason, my boat guests didn't seem too concerned or worried—of course, they hadn't done anything. But having the FBI chasing you for any reason should make one nervous. I decided to go down to Georgetown further down the island chain. I really didn't want to head outward bound for who knows where without Judy. She could always get away, but not without causing problems. I needed to go somewhere safe to think things out and figure a way to call Judy and talk.

I needed to know what they told her, but I couldn't call Grandma's house, that was for certain. Perhaps Judy didn't want to continue this adventure—I sure wouldn't blame her. How did they find Judy's folks? She said Grandma's bank never came up. Nothing was even in the paper about that one. So where was the heat coming from?

Judy remembers: He was calling me and calling me and calling me and wanting me to come, but I wasn't coming because he was still on the same damn boat. The FBI was all around me, and I wasn't going to go. Until that time they couldn't prove anything on me, but if I went back to the boat they would've had all they needed. Besides, I knew what was going to happen.

A few days later, I was sitting in an outdoor bar overlooking the bay of Elizabeth harbor. My passengers were off on a hike somewhere. I noticed some official looking guy with a couple of uniformed cops talking to a fisherman at his little boat and pointing out into the bay where my sailboat was. Sure enough, the cops got in the fisherman's boat and headed toward my boat. My stomach jerked, but I had to see this through. I had nowhere to go without that boat. I got in my dingy and took off to my boat as well.

We arrived at the boat at the same time. The head guy was very polite and wanted to know where the owner was. I told him that would be me.

"What's your name?" I gave him my new Florida license. He said, "I'm the D.E.A. agent for the Bahamas. I got a tip this boat is full of cocaine."

"Who told you that?" I asked.

"The FBI in Miami sent me a bulletin."

"I don't have any cocaine on this boat, sir," I said. I wasn't happy about the search, but I knew the only thing on board was a little pot. And it was probable that Steve and Sally had taken that with them.

"We're going to search it, just in case you aren't telling the truth," he said with a smile.

I shrugged and took a seat in the cockpit with the heavy. The two uniformed guys went down below and, from the sound, started to look everywhere. The D.E.A. guy examined my license as if he believed it was fake or something. After two long searches, they came up empty, but the agent told them to keep searching.

As the D.E.A. man was leaning forward, talking to the cops down the hatch, the wind blew the papers on his clipboard. As the pages fluttered, I saw my real name on one sheet. I was beginning to really worry.

It was about then that a cop, looking very pale, came up the ladder holding a small white towel—inside it was my hand grenade. That surprised everyone—including me.

Once the D.E.A. agent caught his breath, he asked, "Did you declare this before coming into the country?"

"I honestly forgot I had it. A friend gave it to me sometime back to ward off pirates."

He shook his head. I bet the whole thing made his day. "You're under arrest for violating the Bahamas' firearm laws."

Judy remembers: Steve gave it to Les for "protection from pirates." Bullshit! He was thrilled to have a grenade. He was planning on going out in the big wah-wah to make a big splash! I wasn't even there, but I knew what that was about.

I was handcuffed, and assisted into the fisherman's boat, then we headed back to shore. On the way to the police station, they spotted Steve and Sally and arrested them, too. They locked us up in a cell that looked more like a shed while they called Nassau to find out what to do.

The cops took their time coming back. It was decided, since no one could get the radio phone to work, they would take us back to Nassau. We were taken up to the shabby airstrip where a white pilot was sitting in the shade of his Cessna. That was the sky taxi from Nassau. There were the three of us, and there were four of them, plus the pilot—the plane only held six. Two people were going to have to wait for the next plane. Again they had another lengthy conversation as they seemed to get confused about everything.

Still handcuffed, I managed to get next to the pilot and get his attention. I told him, "The head cop over there has a hand grenade in that silver attaché case. As a fellow pilot, I wouldn't fly with a hand grenade from the Korean era—who knows how stable a thirty-year-old hand grenade will be up in a vibrating plane?"

Together we assaulted the chief with our refusals to fly with the attaché contents. Then we had real Bahamian confusion, when the uniformed police overheard our conversation. The pilot said he was leaving and didn't want any part of the whole thing since he was a taxi and not part of the police department. The chief didn't want to be stuck there with three prisoners and no real jail, so he was having a fit trying to keep it all together. In the meantime, bystanders were surrounding the Jeep, trying to figure out what all the commotion was about.

I saw the ruckus as my opportunity to make more problems for the chief. I told him, "If you want to solve the problem, you should get rid of that dangerous grenade! There's no real reason to endanger everyone with certain death if that thing blows up while we're in the air."

The chief seemed interested. "How do we get rid of it?"

I said, "You need to throw it in the ocean. That way nobody'll get hurt. It's the only real way to dispose of it safely."

"How?" he asked. I knew I had him at that point!

"You need to throw it off the dock," I said.

"No," he said. "We'll have the fisherman take it out to the deep water."

Better yet! I was smiling deep inside.

The Jeep driver took one of the cops to the dock. They convinced a fisherman to take them out into the deep water in the bay. One of the cops threw it over the side, not making any attempt to position himself to find it again. Finally, six of us piled into the old Cessna and took off for Nassau. The entire group was pleased with the outcome of the day—especially me!

In Nassau, things got back to formal police work, and we were fingerprinted. I tried very hard to smudge as much as I could, but they used the FBI fingerprint card that wasn't good for me.

The next six days, we found ourselves separated. Steve was with me, but Sally was somewhere else in the stinky jail. I managed to get someone on the other side of the solid wood door to call the U.S. Embassy. The next day, someone came down to see us. The embassy guy said the only reason he came down was that we weren't being charged with a drug crime. If we'd been charged with drugs we would have been on our own. I told him that we needed a lawyer, so he showed us a list, because he couldn't recommend one. I picked one, and some hours later a black attorney with a Cockney accent showed up. He helped me get some food and drink first, then we checked on Sally's safety, and then we got down to business.

He broke out laughing when he heard how I managed to get rid of the evidence against me. He assured me that I'd be in front of a judge the next day. He knew nothing of the FBI involvement.

The next morning, the charges against my passengers were dropped. Only I faced charges that day. I'd never seen an English-style court before—and I must admit I found the whole thing surreal. The court was filled with black people wearing ill-fitting white-powdered wigs. The judge's desk was high up over everyone else, and a box that rose two feet was in the center for me to stand on, flanked by two officers, with my lawyer on my right and the government on my left. The proceedings started by the government's representative giving a very long and damning speech to the court. The word terrorist wasn't in everyday parlance then, but I was the equivalent of one there.

Finally my lawyer got to talk, and he started a long-winded speech too. He suddenly stopped though, and the quiet caught the judge's attention. The judge was a pleasant lady who didn't say much while she was perched way up in the air looking down on the common people, and she came alive by the change in the mood of the room. My lawyer then took over and did his part.

He commended the government on their fine speech, but what he really wanted to see from the government was the evidence. "Where is this hand grenade that everyone has seen but me?" he asked.

The judge looked at the government's table and asked the same question. The government deferred to the chief, who was sitting at the end of the table.

He stood up and told the court, "For the purpose of safety, it was thrown into the sea."

"You threw the evidence into the sea?" the judge asked.

"Yes, your honor."

She turned to the government table and asked, "Is there any evidence against the defendant that is in this court room today?"

The government lawyer repeated, "For the safety of all concerned, the evidence was destroyed."

"This is a waste of the court's time," the judge said. "Case dismissed."

Then the government lawyer spoke up, saying I should be forced to leave the country for the firearm violation. After a lot of talk, it was decided I was to be deported.

I got a chance to talk to the judge before they took me out. I reminded her that I was taken off my yacht and the boat had been wide open for several days with absolutely nobody watching over it and its contents.

She listened and then said, "You're lucky about the evidence. It's clear you've violated the firearm laws of the Bahamas. As such, you must be deported by law. However, you may return on the next flight to claim your boat." With that, I was taken to the airport.

Things were not going well. The FBI had to have my fingerprints by then. They were probably waiting to see what the Bahamian courts did before getting involved. I didn't want to fly to Miami, right into their hands!

The Nassau airport is not real big. One side of the airport was for domestic and the other side was foreign planes. In the center was a lobby with a restaurant at one end. Steve and Sally were there, as they were being deported as well. While we waited for my lawyer to arrive, we got a table at the restaurant and talked about our problems. Nothing about a bank had come up, so I told them they were cool. Just don't tell anyone. I decided to try to get over to the domestic side where about twenty air taxis waited for the next incoming flight. I figured if I could just get over to that side, I could jump on one and fly to my boat. I'd be on the high seas before dark.

When my lawyer showed up, I told him my plan. He told me I needed to bribe the guard to let me out the door. My lawyer went up to the guy and came back to say the guard needed his boss' permission, so my lawyer went to find him. He came back and told me that I could get through for $2 thousand. Great! I gave him $2 thousand, and he left to talk to the guy at the gate. I was ready to go.

I heard the announcement for the incoming flight from Miami. My lawyer told me things were delayed because the damned head of immigration had gone to lunch. But he would keep trying to find him—I shouldn't worry. Then he left.

A half an hour later, a United flight came in. I was sitting at that table with my friends feeling cornered. I watched the entrance from the plane. Three men in suits stepped out—they were very obviously cops. They walked right over to me. The first guy said, "Hi, Les."

I knew it was over, but I asked, "What interest do you have in me?"

He said, "There's a bank in the Keys and a few more we need to talk about. We have a seat on a flight in thirty minutes."

I knew they had jurisdiction to arrest me there. I couldn't think of anything to do but sit there. At least they weren't interested in my friends. I could see by their eyes that Steve and Sally were scared shitless by then. We didn't have time for a lot of goodbyes. I wished them well.

On the plane, I was hemmed in by two FBI guys, and although I wasn't handcuffed, I couldn't have a drink either. I had about $7,000 in my pockets. I realized that once I was in the U.S. I'd lose it to the cops. With a bank robbery charge I was destined to lose all the money I had.

There was a real nice gray-haired woman in the seat in front of me—her seat was back so I could talk to her. I asked, "Ma'am,

WANTED BY THE FBI

BANK ROBBERY; INTERSTATE TRANSPORTATION OF STOLEN PROPERTY; FRAUD BY WIRE

LESLIE ISBEN ROGGE

DESCRIPTION

Born, March 8, 1940; Seattle, Washington; Height, 5'11"; Weight, 160 pounds; Build, medium; Hair, brown (greying); Eyes, blue; Complexion, medium; Race, White; Nationality, American; Scars and Marks, Sea horse on left shoulder, Eagle on right shoulder, Dragon on left shoulder, Devil with word "Les" on right forearm, and may also have a peacock on one arm; Occupations, carpenter, expert recreational sailor, machinist; Remarks, Rogge may have a police scanner in his possession. He wears Foster Grant dark wire-rimmed glasses. He has previously owned and operated large sailboats and has sailed extensively off the coast of Mexico; Social Security Numbers Used, ███████████████████████. He also may be traveling with his wife, Judy Kay Wilson, date of birth, June 28, 1955, Height 5'7", 135 pounds, brown eyes, brown hair, Social Security Number Used, ███████████. WILSON IS ALSO WANTED BY LAW ENFORCEMENT AUTHORITIES.

CAUTION

ROGGE, AN ESCAPEE FROM CUSTODY, IS BEING SOUGHT FOR A SERIES OF BANK ROBBERIES IN WHICH A HANDGUN WAS USED. CONSIDER ARMED AND EXTREMELY DANGEROUS AND AN ESCAPE RISK.

Original wanted poster from 1985 courtesy of D. Ray Barker.

if I gave you some money, would you give it to my wife? These guys are kidnapping me."

She looked at me very concerned, and whispered to the men beside me, "Is he telling me the truth?"

The guy beside me said, "We're FBI, Ma'am. This man is in our custody. But I guess you can take his money."

I handed her all my money and she wrote Judy's phone number down.

We were the last off the plane, and I was arrested as my feet touched the ground. "Welcome home" they told me.

The papers wrote: "A fugitive was arrested while returning from a vacation in the Bahamas."

In prison today, Les builds exact scale models of the sailboats he's owned. For example, a 40' long boat is approximately 40" in length. They are made completely of materials that he can gather inside the prison, like Popsicle sticks from the fudge bars that he can buy in the prison store. Les must eat himself sick of fudge bars, since the entire upper deck on the boats are made of those sticks. They're stained to look just like the deck of a wooden boat. The metal parts of the sailboat are made from aluminum soda cans, string is used for rope, old clothing or napkins for sails. The rudders function with a turn of the steering wheel. His component creations are individually painted—which makes the detail incredible. Getting his creations out of the prison is another feat. He creates his own shipping boxes that have supports on the inside to cradle the fragile sailboat during shipment. There are official procedures for prisoners who want to ship materials out from the prison, and sometimes it has taken Les up to four months to ship a boat after its completion. Just getting it through the system unharmed is a real challenge, but all three of his boats that I have seen have made it across country just fine. They are quite amazing.

Gone Fishin'

*T*his was a hard period for both Les and Judy. When you live in the moment it's hard to plan for the future. After all the banks he robbed, they still didn't have any reserves. It was hard to carry money while he was running from the law. He was financially uneducated about things like off-shore banking or hiding reserves to help themselves for when times got rough. So when Les was incarcerated, they had to rely on the kindness of strangers and his luck.

In June 1984, I was processed into a cell in a federal holding facility. Since the arrest had come quickly, including the deportation, I had no communication with Judy and no lawyer. The Miami Corrections facility did have phones, so as soon as they let me, I called Judy and she started toward Miami. My first worry was the boat. A sailboat sitting at anchor with no activity meant nobody was home—an open invitation to theft. I had no idea what the status of my inflatable was.

Judy showed up and tried to find an attorney. She only had limited funds, since the lady on the plane I gave the money to never contacted her. I needed two lawyers: one for me and another for the boat. My criminal attorney was a man by the name of Nameroff. He was very professional and kept me updated on all that was going on. Doug Skinner was the maritime lawyer. He helped Judy get some wheels, a job and a place to stay.

Judy remembers: I was in Miami, staying in this sleazy motel with no money and Les needed two lawyers—fast. So I simply started dialing down the phone book. The first lawyer I talked to told me I had to have a maritime lawyer and to call these people. They wanted $10 thousand for their services before they even knew the problems involved. At another firm, a guy told me they'd just had an attorney leave the firm to start his own practice and I should give him a call. So I called Doug Skinner and told him what was happening. He asked if I had any money. I told him I didn't, but he asked me to come see him anyway. He took it upon himself to help me: he gave me a job as a legal secretary for about five months while Les was getting ready for trial; gave me money to buy clothes; and loaned me a car. He was simply a great guy. I mean, I can't say that about any other lawyer!

The manager of the bank, the woman who had stared at me intensely, was highly outraged that anyone would dare rob her bank and was at the center of the case against me in Florida. Her boyfriend was an FBI agent, and the two of them decided that they could seize my boat as proceeds of the crime against them, and could then end up with the boat themselves. Who would know?

They found a worker who knew the boat well enough to sail it. The guy worked at a marina where I'd stayed in the past. They gave him $2,500 to go to the Bahamas and steal the boat. Of course, the FBI knew all the details of where the boat was and the pair used that information to their benefit. They didn't have jurisdiction to put a lien on the boat while it was out of the country, so it had to be in the U.S. for their plan to work. Since I hadn't been convicted of robbery yet, they were actually guilty of

Mr. Tambourine Man in 1983 after Les's escape

conspiracy to commit international theft and illegally smuggling stolen property into the U.S. without declaring it. The FBI agent thought he was above the law. Their plan didn't work, but it did bring my boat back to the States.

Meanwhile, I was going through the motions of bail hearings and court appearances with Nameroff, Judy and Skinner every week. The first step was to claim jurisdiction in Florida so we could get the boat back to the U.S. and away from the cops who were being paid by the bank to guard it. At first, Judy wasn't allowed to board the boat, but after a while she got the OK from the courts and was able to get her personal items. She also managed to get the electronics.

The government's lawyer's name was Ms. Kunt, and our lawyer would mispronounce her name on purpose to the point where she almost had a fit. She lost and jurisdiction went to Admiralty Court—Skinner's home court. Judy was able to sell the boat to a lawyer, and then we had money to pay our lawyer fees that were totaling about $25 thousand. We also ended up paying for the money I stole in the bank, which was all we had.

Sometime later, the FBI agent and the bank manager were indicted for various crimes, which came at a bad time for me. The only witness to the bank robbery was the manager, who claimed about $40 thousand was taken by a Latino who was five-foot-seven or -eight with black hair, a dark complexion and clean-shaven. I, of course, am five-foot-ten with blue eyes, a bushy beard and a new driver's license in another name, but showing a full beard. The marina operator testified I had gray hair, blue eyes and a beard at that time. My lawyer said he thought we had a clear lack of identification.

Things were looking good: the boat was gone, but we could never have operated it in the U.S. again after her history and the FBI involvement. Another boat could always be had, but freedom could not.

In this country, if you plead not guilty and don't take the plea deal the D.A. offers, you need to be ready to accept a higher penalty if you lose—give the D.A. a conviction or place yourself at the maximum side of punishment if the jury doesn't rule in your favor. We decided not to take the plea deal.

At my trial, the manager was facing all of her problems with the boat, and she had to take the stand and under oath tell the court, "I don't care what I told the FBI about the description of the robber, that man there is the person who robbed me!" She pointed at me. The jury came back with a quick guilty verdict. Because I hadn't accepted the plea deal, after about a month, the judge gave me twenty years, and off to the penitentiary in Lewis-burg, Pennsylvania I went.

Judy stayed on in Miami to help Skinner file charges against the FBI agent and the manager. We worked up a suit against the FBI and the government for the agent's actions under the cover of his badge. Skinner said it would take four to five years to wind through the courts, but it was the most detailed case against an agent of the FBI he'd ever heard about, short of a murder case.

Judy and I (and the lawyers) were due many thousands of dollars from that legal action, but I would unknowingly screw up the entire case later.

After four months in Lewisburg, the FBI's dominos were starting to fall. My next court date was in Moscow, Idaho, for a bank robbery I committed in Post Falls, Idaho, in 1981. I heard that they were planning on trying me for close to nine bank robberies that I'd committed in the West, so after the Idaho trial I'd be taken to other states. The U.S. Marshals picked me up and we flew to Salt Lake City, Utah, and drove the rest of the way. For some reason, and I never understood why, the state of Utah was mad at the Marshals for coming through their state. After a night in the SLC county jail, we drove north to Idaho with an escort all the way to the border for whatever reason.

Arriving at the Latah County jail in Moscow (the county seat), I was placed in a special section for federal prisoners. It had a little lockdown section with a table, shower, television and some sleeping cells to wait for trial. I was given a court-appointed trial lawyer named D. Ray Barker, and he was great. He recommended a trial by judge after reviewing all of the evidence, but there ended up being a jury anyway. He claimed that the specific judge for the trial was a stickler for the facts.

In an interview in August of 2008, Barker recounted: When I was appointed in Les's federal case, I was given a discovery packet that included all the police reports and all the information that the FBI had put together. It included the bank robbery in Post Falls, Idaho, but there was also information on ten other bank robberies all over the Pacific and the West they were sure he'd committed. The plan was to try him in Idaho and then move him to California, Arizona, Nevada and all the other states, so they could try him in these other cases.

Les's attorney, Mr. D. Ray Barker, in Moscow, Idaho. August, 2008.

I remember going through one of them with him one day, and he said, "Yeah, I really screwed up on that one."

I said, "What do you mean?"

He said, "Well, I got in the bank and was ready to start my thing, and I looked across the counter and the lady looking at me lived in the same apartment complex as me. We knew each other."

The 1981 Idaho bank robbery was the last one I'd committed with someone else. The guy was a Mexican from Los Angeles who I knew in McNeal prison in the '60s. He ended up getting caught in California for another crime, and ratted on me for a reduced sentence. Barker got a copy of his statement to the FBI, where he told them who was with him on the Idaho robbery.

The question was whether he would testify against me. We had to find out his plan so we could figure out how to handle my case. If he was planning on testifying, it was a no-brainer to make the best deal we could. Barker talked to the guy's wife and asked her to ask him if he was planning to testify in court. She said she would. Being a rat in the federal system was a big problem—you can't hide and the other prisoners don't like that sort of behavior. His wife got back to Barker, and I wasn't surprised to hear that he wouldn't testify. So off to trial we went.

When I was with Les, he was very proud of the fact that no one had ever been hurt in any of his crimes, Barker said. Les was probably the most articulate federal defendant I ever had, and he could tell a story. He told lots of stories when I spent time with him in the jail.

Once Les told me, "I'm going to tell you how to rob a bank." OK, I'll play this. He said, "What you do is go get yourself a real nice three-piece suit and a real nice expensive briefcase, and you walk into the bank and ask to see the manager and they always usher you into the manager's office. You very pleasantly and quietly tell the manager that he is to take the briefcase and fill it up with money, and then you leave."

I said, "That sounds real good, but what if he says no?"

He said, "You grab your briefcase and run like hell!"

During all of my court appearances, I was watched by a young U.S. Marshal named Bob. When he pulled night duty, he would usually bring a chair back and sit outside of my cage area and we'd talk or watch television. From start to sentencing in the federal system, the process can take months and perhaps as much as a year and a half if there's a trial. Then there's a sentencing period if you're found guilty—most of the cases brought to trial in federal courts conclude with a guilty verdict. The case was over four years old, had one witness who was the manager, and a kid who was sixteen at the time who was outside the bank and witnessed the getaway. The co-defendant wouldn't testify, so we were looking good. I was hoping that if the case was dismissed, the government would be satisfied with the twenty year sentence I already had.

Bob was there for every court appearance, so he was intimately informed of all of the details of the case. The day of the trial, my lawyer came back with some clothes for me to wear, but they weren't mine. I had a sport coat and pants, but he had a new grey suit and a red tie. *Great,* I thought, *this looks good. Now this is a good lawyer.*

Barker recalled: I had an intern, a law student named John Hathaway, and he had a part-time job while he went to law school, working at the sheriff's office at the jail. He became acquainted with Rogge, but he was not the one who helped him. He and Les became friends in the jail, and John's wife, who was a beautician, came in and did Les's hair before the trial—that's how informal things were. John at that time had whitish hair and was sitting on one side of me (in the courtroom), and Les was kind of graying, too, and was sitting on the other side of me. They did look something alike, if you weren't paying attention.

The bailiff brought in the bank manager through a door on the side of the courtroom. The prosecutor was standing in front of the witness box waiting for the former bank manager to come in. He didn't notice Barker had John and I switch places. Barker whispered that this witness needed to make a positive I.D., and sure enough the prosecutor drilled his only witness about the details. He swung his arm to point at our table—but didn't check to see who was sitting where.

After what felt like an hour, the prosecutor finally asked with great drama, "Can you identify the robber of the bank today?"

"I can," she answered.

"And would you point him out to the court?" he asked the witness.

"That man," she said—pointing at John!

I was dying inside—I couldn't believe it was happening the way Barker planned!

The D.A. went on hammering out his perfect answer without seeing that the wrong man had been indicated. Finally, he turned and realized he'd been tricked. He stammered and yelled, "These sorts of shenanigans don't belong in the courtroom!"

Although I didn't know it at the time, Barker had told the judge what he planned to do. The D.A. and Barker shouted objections at each other while the witness was recovering, and the judge pounded his gavel. I looked behind me, and there were quite a few people sitting in the seats smiling and joking.

Barker asked for an acquittal on the grounds of lack of identification of the accused.

The judge said that he would rule later, and had the prosecutor call his next witness. He was the driver of the Jeep that followed us away from the bank. Here's what happened: There were two teenagers in an open Jeep that had a large C.B. radio antenna waving in the back. They happened to be driving by the bank when the manager came running out into the main street yelling as we pulled away in our getaway car. The kids turned around and followed us. We had driven the getaway car to a parking lot of the post office out of sight of this main street and changed cars. As we pulled through the parking lot exit, we saw the kids coming down the street.

I had a weak little .38 automatic on me that I never intended to use on anyone, but I had to stop the kids with their C.B. radio from following us, since they'd seen the second car. I leaned out the passenger-side window and tried to blow out their windshield, just like in the movies. Only I'd never fired that gun before, and it wasn't the movies, so I ended up shooting out the driver's side front tire by accident. At least that stopped the Jeep, and we were up on the freeway and out of town. Post Falls was right on the Washington-Idaho border, and we headed west to Washington where my pickup and camper were at a rest area. On the scanner, the police chased a car that they believed robbed the bank going *east*, so we got away.

In the court room four years later, the driver, who was now twenty years old, told his story. The prosecutor tried to make an attempted murder case, but the kid didn't go for it. Not only couldn't he identify me, but he said two to three times that, "The robbers were very professional. They could have shot me or my buddy at any time, but they only shot out my tire to stop us." So the government didn't get any points out of that witness. Good kid.

More courtroom navigating went on, but the trial was basically over. The judge then ruled—to the surprise of everyone there—that the bank manager's misidentification was a harmless error.

And then he found me guilty.

Barker said: The thing that ended up convicting him was, even without the identification, they could prove that his fingerprints were in the getaway car. Not much you can do about that.

When I was taken back to the jail, Bob couldn't believe what had happened. He'd sat through the entire thing, and was sure the outcome would be not guilty. I think he was more upset than anyone—including me! He told me that the judge was a fair guy and I should expect a sentence that reflected that.

After a pre-sentence report that had been copied directly from the Miami sentence report, the judge called me back and gave me two more twenty-year sentences, added to my Florida sentence. Now I had a total of sixty years!

Barker said: They gave him two twenty-year sentences, one for each teller. I thought that was wrong. But even if we had a successful appeal, he still would have had one twenty-year sentence.

After the sentencing, Bob and I talked about freedom and that it was worth all you had. I told him I had $50 thousand buried in L.A., and that I would gladly give it to anyone who would help me.

Bob was off Friday and Saturday, but on Sunday morning he returned to work and he asked, "If I help you escape, can I have the $50,000?"

"Of course," I said.

He told me, "I'm going to get permission to move you into the law library—which has a fire door in the back. I'll go get your court clothes."

I couldn't believe what I was hearing. "Can you call a friend of mine and have him pick me up about noon?"

"Sure," he said. "Give me the number." I did and he left.

I wondered: *Is this for real, or am I being set up by the FBI for their bother in Miami?* Whatever the deal, I knew that once I got to the penitentiary it would be too late to think about running. It had to happen now!

Bob returned with my court clothes. "Pack your stuff. I'll move you to the library in fifteen minutes."

I dressed so fast, I had ten minutes to spare. The only personal items I had were some big brown envelopes, but I had on my suit and looked good. I was pretty sure I could walk away from there if the ride didn't come. While I was waiting, I grabbed my felt tip marker and made a sign. Then I put it on the table.

Bob unlocked the cell door, and we went to the library. He explained that the fire door exited right out on the lawn of the side street. He gave me the key, and told me to go ahead and unlock it. That way I could wait for my ride to drive up.

I told him, "I'll scratch up the lock—but it probably won't fool anyone for long." Then I tried to tell him what to expect from the government.

He put up a hand to stop me. "I can handle it. Now, don't forget to send me the money!"

At noon, I was peeking out a crack in the door and losing hope for my ride. I was just starting to plan how I would walk downtown and find a car to steal—when a sedan pulled up and stopped. It was my pal! I got in and thanked him.

He said, "I'm taking you to Missoula, Montana, about 150 miles through these mountains on Highway 12."

I said, "Great! Thanks. Please don't speed. And do you think we can stop and get a six-pack of beer and some smokes?" *I'm free! Just like that—I'm free! It's unbelievable!*

I gulped three beers down, sat back and enjoyed the ride. It was getting dark when we pulled into west Missoula and found a little motel. He gave me forty dollars—which was another surprise—and rented me a room. I gave him a big hug, and then he left.

I'm free!

Barker said: When he escaped, I was very, very surprised that it could happen, that it did happen. Later, I kind of just smiled to myself—I wasn't devastated. I was called immediately,

Latah County Jail escape door, now with surveillance. 2008.

and I was up at the sheriff's office within five minutes. There was every law enforcement agency there; the Feds, the county, the city, Fish and Game. I don't recall now if the Forest Service was there, he said smiling. He was our favorite subject here. Les was so memorable that we named our dog Rogge. Stories went on for years. The Marshals would give me updates.

After I got settled, I realized I had three beers left and about eight bucks, so first I needed some money. I started walking toward downtown Missoula that was about fifteen blocks, but I was still high from the freedom, so I didn't mind the walk. I knew I looked respectable, and doubted the alarm had traveled as far as Missoula yet. I found a mall with a bank of pay phones, so I started dialing for dollars. People were very forthcoming, and one offered to wire me some money—everything was going my way!

In all of my years in my career of robbing banks, changing identities, moving around and meeting new people, Judy and I met people who never disowned us when they learned the truth about us. We were still good friends, and most of these people would surprise me by not turning me in for the rewards. Twice that I can remember, people put themselves at risk to warn us about the police looking for me.

I spent my last few dollars on a fast food place where I had the best and most greasy hamburger I'd ever had. Then I started walking again and discovered a nice, big Volvo-Chevy dealer. I didn't know how much money I would be able to assemble, so I figured a car wouldn't be in the budget. I didn't have a driver's license, so getting stopped was a problem whether the car was hot or not. The car lot was nicely spread out without any guards or chains across the driveways. It was definitely the spot to shop that night, but it was much too early, since I didn't have any gas money.

Since I didn't have any I.D., the fat, bossy Western Union lady demanded I show the panther tattoo on my arm as proof I was who I said I was. I'd asked three people to send whatever they could without using credit cards that would mark them down the road for helping me. I really didn't know if I would get $200 or $2,000, but it really didn't matter much after the first couple of hundred. Right then, anything would have gotten me on the road and out of the area. I was worried that Missoula was in the Moscow, Idaho, television area. I didn't know how much press my escape would generate.

The clerk asked, "How much are you expecting?"

I told her, "However much they love me." I had no idea of the total from the three different senders.

She fooled around with her computer for five more minutes, and said, "You have $3,000 coming in. I'll write you a check."

"A check isn't going to be any good to me. This is an emergency and I need the money tonight. My people sent me cash, and that's what I want."

Gone Fishin'

She told me that her safe was locked, and so forth. I told her to call her manager. She didn't want to bother him at night, but I reminded her they were a twenty-four-hour operation. I didn't have any more money to go sit in a bar or a restaurant, and it was a long walk back to the motel. I needed to get the car that night. After about a half-hour, she yelled to me that her boss was coming in to open the safe. He was scared that there was going to be a robbery or something.

At about midnight, I finally got my money and was off in the night. It was always a good feeling to have money in the pocket. Money isn't freedom, but it can provide freedom to move.

I started back toward the car dealership. Traffic was very thin, and a couple of times cops passed me without a second look. It was cold, and I didn't have an overcoat. I had forgotten to buy one when I saw the mall and was planning my night. I didn't like to travel much at night on a freeway in the very early hours of the morning, since you really stand out—who in their right mind would be out at that time of night? But tonight I had to travel at least a hundred miles away.

At the dealership, I walked all around looking for cameras and alarms, but found nothing. Even the lights were pointed in my favor, shining out on the cars away from the showroom. The backdoor to the showroom from the service department was glass and didn't have an alarm on it that I could see. I used a cinder block I kicked off the nearby planter box to break out the bottom half of the door. I drifted back out of the way to await any sort of reaction, and when nothing happened I crawled through the door and across the showroom floor to the sales manager's office. Once I was around the corner and in front of his desk, it all looked very familiar. The center drawer had keys to a few cars—probably the ones he had deals working on. I saw a Volvo turbo wagon, a Caprice, a couple of Chevys and a Toyota hatchback that was a year old. The Toyota was run-of-the-mill, so I took the set of keys thinking it would be reliable. The right desk drawer held the treasure: blank contracts, rental agreements and temporary license plates. I was in business in case I got stopped on the way out of town.

With my stolen stuff, I left back through the broken door, snatched a dealer's plate off of the Volvo, put it on the Toyota, and got in. A quick twist of the key showed I had a quarter of a tank of gas and a smooth running engine—then I was praying for heat. I pulled out and headed for the motel. It was dark and quiet as I pulled up to the room. Inside, I quickly made up a set of temporary tags. I made out a sales contract with a nice pen from the manager's office, folded it and placed it in an envelope—also borrowed. It all looked very right. Then I went outside and put the temporary plates on the Toyota.

I headed out on Highway 90 to Wyoming. I drove for three days, stopping and eating good food, drink and making discreet phone calls to get up to speed. I heard that heads were rolling in Moscow and at the U.S. Marshall's office. The day I'd escaped was the day the Marshall's office was planning on transporting the fugitives from the courts to the prison, so I barely made it. The FBI was helping, since a crime had been committed, but it was the Marshall's responsibility when someone left their custody. It didn't happen often, but when it did, blame went down the ladder. Poor Bob had told me he could handle the investigation, and I'm sure he did—for about twenty minutes. He was charged for his crime.

Mr. Barker laughed his ass off when he told me the reaction of a newsperson taking photos of my cell area and got a picture of the sign I'd left. He told me he really liked my case and wished me good luck, but he also told me not to call back as he was sure his phone was bugged.

What did the sign say?

GONE FISHIN'

Gone Fishin'

Barker added: When Bob was on trial, we received a letter from Les, posted from Europe. We suspect he sent it to somebody in Europe, and they sent it back. It explained that Bob hadn't done anything wrong, that Les had picked the lock himself, a skill he knew very well. It was an attempt to help Bob. Bob did spend some time in jail for his actions.

I was sure the FBI and the U.S. Marshals were also all over Judy like white on rice. They were probably parked at the end of her folk's driveway in Lake Charles. I was sure it was going to be hard to get away from them, but I was also sure we would find a way. She'd promised to cook me a Thanksgiving dinner somewhere, and I was going to get it!

America's Most Wanted

*M*y mother visited Les the day before he escaped. I was fifteen at the time, and drove my mother from Portland to see Les in the jail. We got into town and found a motel on Friday, then went to visit Les on Saturday morning. I didn't get to see him since I was less than sixteen-years-old. Mum enjoyed her visit, although it was difficult to see her brother behind bars. We left that same morning, heading for home. On Monday afternoon, we got a knock on our door and there stood the FBI. Les had escaped on Sunday. Mum had good timing, since the next time she saw Les was in 1998, when she again visited him in prison, this time in Texas.

I knew they were looking for me, and I knew I couldn't contact any of my family, including Troy or Tracy. I decided to visit some old friends that Judy and I had met coming down the Mississippi River. I was pretty sure the FBI knew nothing about these people. One such friend was Little David who visited us on *Mr. T* in Mexico.

I called his number, but didn't get an answer. So I drove over to the Lake Ferguson club and there he was sitting at the bar. He was very surprised and gave me a huge hug. He explained that the news about who I really was had come out. Everyone knew about the bank robbery in Florida, so hanging around there wasn't a good idea. He showed me a hotel that didn't ask questions, and we partied for a couple of days. I went over and saw my old show truck that I missed so much. It still looked great.

I told Little David goodbye and headed to South Louisiana to catch up with Judy and get a place to stay. I needed some new I.D., as well. I ended up hooking up with some of Judy's friends who lived in Alexandra, a couple of hours drive north of Judy's parents' place. I dumped the Toyota with the keys in a bad neighborhood—it was gone before sunset.

I had a friend tell Judy to go to the Wal-Mart every day. "Take Floyd, if you like, but make sure you go every day. Call me when the cops stop following you." At ten a.m. every morning, she would go in, shop and leave.

My money was getting real low. I bought a realistic-looking plastic gun, a shooter-holster and an old hand-held scanner at a hock shop near Fort Polk that had all the local frequencies in it. I paid a young kid to steal an old pickup for me. Then I made arrangements for my friend to pick me up at a restaurant near the gates of Fort Polk. I drove onto the base and robbed the bank there. As I was waiting for the vault clerk to deliver the bag o' money to the manager's office, it struck me that I was surrounded by all of these Army guys with weapons, and here I was with my little plastic gun. I never had to produce the gun, other than show a glimpse of the handle under my coat. The robbery went very well, and I ended up clearing about $45 thousand.

I dumped the old pickup and purchased an older Cadillac, moved to a better place, got a driver's license in another name, insurance papers and I was all set—except that Judy was still being followed every day.

It was the second week in November, and I'd escaped on September 29th. It had been about six weeks, and they were serious about keeping an eye on Judy. They must have known all that we'd been through and the fact that I wasn't going anywhere without her. Then our luck changed. They got lazy and stopped going into Wal-Mart. I told Judy to keep it up, and when she saw them stay in the car five times in a row call a cab to meet her in the back of the store and walk straight through and away.

Judy remembers: They didn't get lazy. They sat at the entrance to the bridge at the end of my road and waited for me to come out, and then followed me everywhere I went. I went to Wal-Mart with my brother, Larry, who'd just got out of prison. FBI agents stopped us in the parking lot. They searched the car and told me I'd better turn around and go home and stay there. That's when I knew I had to leave. This went on for three weeks. I guess they got tired of following me, because the last time they pulled us over in the parking lot, I simply said OK and headed home. Half-way there, I noticed they weren't behind me. So I went to a friend's house. She knew where Les was and took me to him. We stayed a week on Toledo Dam and laid low in a cabin. I tried to find my friend again, but couldn't. I would love to see them again. I also never did see Larry again. He died while we were on the run; he died the wrong way and way too early.

The FBI and Marshals knew they'd been beaten, but that didn't stop them from bothering Judy's parents and friends. I got my home-cooked turkey dinner, as promised. Then we found out that Doug Skinner had been very close to winning my big civil case against the bank in the Keys, the FBI, their agent and the U.S. Government. But my escape rendered the case moot, and it all just evaporated. Skinner said he was thoroughly disgusted that all his hard work could be blown by such a dumb act. It wasn't dumb to me. I'd do the same thing again—because I was free!

Judy recalls: Skinner wasn't really upset. He would call mother to check in on us. Mother would tell him, "I don't know who you are so I'm not telling you nothin'!"

Getting Judy back was a major accomplishment. Together they had beaten the FBI, again, and it would be another decade before they would really catch up to Les. The escape and relationship with Judy gathered attention from national publications and television shows, one of which was "Unsolved Mysteries." At that time, the show spotlighted hunts for fugitives as well as other phenomena. We knew Les was going to be featured, so we gathered the family to watch the excitement at Mum's. Les has a niece by the name of Lesley, and naturally she is called Les—she wasn't named after Les, but they share the same first and last name. Little Les was very young then, around five or so, and when the host introduced Leslie Rogge, Little Les got really scared and started to cry. It also made me realize how it affected the adults in the immediate family as well. I was always proud of my uncle for some reason. Perhaps I was simply in awe, but I was never embarrassed by him or emotionally stressed either. He was simply my uncle; the one who wasn't normal like in most families. To this day there are still very hard feelings in the family, and most don't have much communication with Les in prison. Perhaps the future will be different.

Little Les is now a graphics artist and designed this book's cover.

Judy and I messed around in South Texas a while, bought a small boat and fixed it up, then headed for the East Coast. When we got to Norfolk, Virginia, we stopped and looked for another boat.

We found a huge trawler built for the Virginia Institute for Marine Science department that had been decommissioned for a newer boat. She was a 57' wooden boat, with a rebuilt 671 die-

Pathfinder at berth in Willoughby Spit after purchase, awaiting refit.

sel engine, that had been built like a tank to survive the rough Chesapeake Bay winters. She'd been stripped and looked like a wooden shrimper, although much different inside. A shrimper has its engine forward in the boat with the central section as a fish hold. The boat's engine was astern of the center leaving the whole center and forward open for accommodations below with two staterooms, a dinette, a galley and an engine room almost full height. The whole on-deck house was open since it was originally the lab. Because nobody kept any fish in the hold, the boat didn't smell like fish. It was an ideal boat to convert to live-aboard.

We got it up and running for about $27 thousand and made it into a beautiful home. Judy did the insides with new paint, carpet and new wallpaper in the galley. We had a trash compactor and an ice machine. I did the mechanical work including adding a new generator and new electronics to the pilot house. I removed the flying bridge and re-sided the house. It took us a total of three years and about $300 thousand to finally get it perfect in the end.

Our boat, *Pathfinder*—the boat's original name—looked so much like a shrimper, sometimes we got the shrimpers' price for fuel.

While at the marina at Willoughby Spit, all that rebuilding ran through our funds quickly. So I left to go back to what I called work. I did treat it like a job—one I had to do right since there were extreme consequences if I messed up. I found work in Eldorado, Arkansas, on February 9th, 1986. I left town with $98 thousand of the local bank's money. Ten years later, I found out it was owned by a judge!

Some say that boats are holes in the water you stuff money in to. It's true they're expensive—but also rewarding to those who love them.

We decided we'd had enough of Virginia when we sold our old Caddy to buy what we called a key cruiser—a throw-away Ford station wagon. Dependability was the only thing that counted, and we picked up one for $400. It took us five days to go from department to department to get a license tag. It seemed everyone wanted to know if all of your taxes were paid up, and if you didn't live in Virginia there was no record of you paying those taxes. After several frustrating days, we finally got the license. We decided to leave Virginia and all of their commonwealth nonsense.

Somehow we got directed to a private little marina, on the Washington River in Bedford County, owned by a great guy who didn't need the money—he just liked his boats. Mr. John liked us and took us in, and that meant we were family. We were invited to all the events that happened every weekend . . . with the weather's approval.

Everything was great until we faced our first hurricane. In August, 1986, Hurricane Charley came ashore. We were forced to leave the marina by policy. Their theory was that boats banging around during a hurricane would damage the marina docks, so all the boats had to leave. We put down our two largest anchors in a way to ride out the shifting winds as the hurricane went past—it was more guesswork than a science. Our plan worked for the first two hours until the wind veered and all of the boat's fifty tons were pulling on one anchor with a 7/8" nylon rope stretching to impossible lengths. With the winds reaching 100 m.p.h., I knew the rope was going to break and we'd be dashed into the rock bulkheads behind us that fronted the Navy base. If that happened, we'd never get the boat off the huge hunks of granite. We had the engine running wide open—something you normally avoid on a new engine. The radio was predicting two more hours, and I was sure we wouldn't be able to hold out that long. Just then, the wind died. We looked at each other—*Now what?* The eye was supposed to have passed, but we weren't sure and had no real way to tell. I throttled down the engine as things got calmer and calmer.

The next day, the scene around us was scary—there was disaster everywhere. Boats had broken their moorings and were upside down all along the shore. Most people had the good sense to anchor their boats as well as they could and leave. We were stupid and cared more for the boat than ourselves and stayed— and that time we were lucky.

Once the storm cleanup was accomplished, we pulled *Pathfinder* out of the water and painted her green. She looked like a yacht. Judy had white Berber carpet installed in the salon and put up a huge awning over the rear deck, while I built a picnic table to match the siding. Things were looking good.

That winter, Judy and I left John's place. Now that the boat was pretty we wanted to go somewhere cool. We headed south down the Ditch (ICW) and stopped at Beaufort, South Carolina. In Beaufort we found this old, broken down shrimp company that had a retail store up on the road that didn't have any boat

Les making *Pathfinder* pretty.

business any longer, so we tied up and walked up to the seafood store and talked the guy into letting us tie up there for a while— we always had good luck at shrimp/fish docks since we looked like an old shrimp boat. Those old fishing farts always said they wanted to do that to their boats.

The old piece of shit dock was a "T" style dock with the "T" being where the boats tied up, and the "I" part of the dock went to land. Our part was the worst. Someone had broken a couple pilings, and the dock had a bad sag in it for about twenty feet or so that tipped toward the water. One morning we woke up to a black ice storm, and everything was coated in a half-inch thick layer of pure ice—including the old wooden dock.

I may sound like a hopeless drunk who drinks a cold beer for breakfast, but that was who I was that day only to wake up to no beer left. That meant a beer run, and it was only a short run across the street from the seafood store. But leaving the boat was very iffy since there was nothing to hang onto, and the drop was about seven feet down to icy water if I slipped. It didn't seem very dangerous, but it would've been cold and wet for sure.

Leaving the boat and walking down the sloped part of the dock took all my concentration, and I thought I was going swimming a couple of times.

Leaving the store I had two twelve-packs of beer and a couple items for Judy. I sure as hell didn't want to do that again tonight. With my groceries, there was only one way to get back to the boat—on my hands and knees. I had the two twelve-packs and a brown paper bag in front of me, and I crawled pushing my bounty along in front. They wanted to slide to the side and right in the drink, so then I was holding onto the beer, one in each hand, and pushing the brown paper bag with my nose.

About this time, the owner wandered down to the good part of the dock right behind me and said, "Look, don't get the wrong idea, but maybe you should come with me to my noon A.A. meeting. It looks like you're going through a lot of trouble for a beer. How about it? Want to ride along? No strings."

I looked back at the ship and saw Judy standing at my goal line on the flat part of the dock next to *Pathfinder*. I believe she was pissing her pants with laughter. She shouted, "Yeah, take the old rummy with you. He needs it by the looks of this!"

It did look bad, but it was out of context.

I ended up going to the AA meeting anyway, and I failed their questioning about if I was an alcoholic:

Do you drink alone?

Do you have black outs?

Have you lost or gotten fired for missing work because of drinking?

Does your wife and kids hate your drinking?

Do you have any D.U.I.s?

Is your liver bad?

On and on the questions came, and my answer was no to all of them!

America's Most Wanted

Before we knew it, we were low on money again. At the time, I was sort of working, delivering boats up and down the East Coast for the rich. I towed boats here and there and stayed relatively busy.

One day, I had to go to High Point, North Carolina—which is where Hatteras built their boats. As I was leaving town, a light caught my eye. Across the street was a mall that had a fairly big First Citizens Bank at the end. It had full-length windows at the front end, and I could see the inside. What really caught my breath was when I saw the curtains closing on these very large windows—my watch showed one p.m. I turned into the mall and drove down toward the end of the bank and parked away from the building. Then I walked up to the front door.

All of the curtains were drawn, and the lettering on the door said they were closed from 1 – 2 p.m. I'd only dreamed of things like that! I drove back to the hotel that I had just stayed in, and called Judy to tell her I'd found work and not to worry, but I was going to be a few days longer.

I already had a plan in my head—I just needed to bring all the details together. Two days later, on July 17th, 1986, I appeared at 12:50 for my 12:30 appointment to see the manager. I'd called to say I was running late, should we reschedule? She told me, "Just come in late, that will be fine." As I was shown into her office I could hear the curtains closing behind me.

By then, I had my system down pat: I put the scanner on the desk with the squelch turned up for a moment to show it was working; my letter of introduction and notice that this was a robbery, instructing her to call the vault clerk over to her office, etc. Once that was done, I had to secure the others—six, I believe—in the coffee room where they'd assembled. I simply unhooked the receiver from the only phone in the room. I told them to enjoy their lunch and not to try to leave until they were told to.

I gave the vault clerk a large nylon bag that folded into nothing from my briefcase and told her if she put anything other than paper in the bag I'd know and wouldn't be happy. "The money is insured, so let's not turn this into a homicide. Let the police do their job," I told her. I also mentioned that I wanted the twenties, fifties and hundreds, all the $50 and $100 American Express travelers checks, all the gold coins and whatever. I had forty-five minutes until lunch was over, so I made the most of it.

It seems almost unbelievable, but I had to make two trips to my car with the bag I brought in and two black trash bags they had. I never thought I'd need more bags! The manager held the front door for me as I took the money first, then the other two bags in a second trip to my trunk. If she'd locked me out, I would still have had the money bag—but she didn't. I drove away, switched to the Ford cruiser and hit the freeway.

I cleared $149 thousand in cash and $409 thousand in blank traveler's checks that we spent every cent of over the next six years—save for two that I signed wrong. I also came away with sixty-nine blank cashier's checks and a bag of gold coin—which was a mighty fine day's work. All of that thanks to those curtains.

Back at the boat, Judy got her white leather sofa.

I believe Les was overconfident at this point in his career. He was going about his business and making friends as if he were a normal citizen. He was still confident about traveling without being noticed, although he continually worked on replacing his I.D. and having backups in case he got stopped by the police. But the newspapers and other syndicated news media were now constantly writing about the robberies—which generated tips as to Les's whereabouts. Les got photographed at every bank he robbed. Although he wore sunglasses and dressed nicely, the FBI and the U.S.

America's Most Wanted

Marshals knew who he was. They were gathering new information and slowly getting closer every day.

We were there a bit under a year, when I committed a big boo-boo trying to be a good guy. Most of the locals used outboards for pulling their crab traps and running back and forth. Everyone had a boat, and the motors were always in demand. The local dealer was the only Johnson-Evenrude dealer around for miles, so he had a lock on the sales and the parts and he was asking full price for everything. One weekend before crab season, these guys were complaining about his prices being too high and their dollars being too short, as always. I thought I needed to get in the middle of that since I saw an opportunity to help those guys and get some money for my own boat project. So I told a few that if they pooled their money, I'd take a trip to see a friend who could get some wholesale prices on a dozen or so new motors. They all wanted the same motors, so it was going to be real easy. At the time, the motors retailed for around $3,500, and I told them that I thought I could get a dozen or so for about $2,700 each. Of course, I didn't know anyone who would wholesale me motors, but that was the easy part. I checked a couple of catalogs and made a few phone calls, and it was all worked out. I bought the motors with one of my cashier's checks—pure profit and everyone was happy—except for the insurance company and the local dealer!

I found with careful stacking that a person could get about fourteen of those forty horsepower Johnsons in a big pickup truck. Of course, I became a hero around town all summer. But the word was out that the story with the motors was a little vague and the prices too good to be true. So they knew not to take the motors in for any warranty work to the local dealer.

Someone bragged about how they'd paid this great price for the motors through a friend, and it got back to the local Evenrude dealer. He was very curious as to who sold those motors so cheap and was cutting into his territory.

One night a local at a bar, one of my customers went out to find the dealer trying to get the engine number off of the boat behind his truck. He promptly ran him off, but let me know about the incident. I decided it was time to move south, and maybe the story would die.

We underestimated the dealer. He finally got a number off one of those motors and called the factory. They told him they were purchased in Florida with a stolen check from a bank.

At that point we'd moved on, and it had been months since the outboard deal. We drifted down to a marina outside of Charleston, South Carolina, where we got a job towing boats that had been seized for drugs—for the D.E.A. of all people!— into storage. I was running the marina yard, so we were living at the dock for free. We had two Mexican laborers helping Judy sand and epoxy the hull for less than I was making, so we were getting the last work on the boat done for next to nothing and really liking our new living.

We ended up doing some real fun jobs for the Coast Guard. Sometimes we would look at each other during a rescue and almost blow a gasket! Here we were, with either the D.E.A. or Customs aboard our boat in charge of towing or whatever, and the FBI was looking all over for me!

At times, we even bought some of the confiscated boats and re-sold them after taking what we wanted off of them first. We usually kept the boats for at least a year at the marina before something happened in the courts.

I remember one time, we had to go to Savanna Georgia Coast Guard station to pick up an 85' steel shrimp boat from Colombia with forty tons of pot on board. They were unloading the pot into U-Haul trucks, and we had to wait. Shit, there was pot everywhere with the plastic bags breaking. We were getting paid $1,500 per hour to tow it back to Charleston on a sixteen hour trip. That night, the D.E.A. agent and I were in the pilot-house drinking beer and telling stories till daylight.

Then, the Customs guys came aboard to sign papers. He told me, "Make sure the boat is clean for storage. Don't forget to remove any hazardous or combustible materials."

"Including the fuel?" I asked. "What the hell am I going to do with 5,000 gallons of diesel fuel?"

The guy asked, "How big are your tanks?"

I told him, "Two thousand gallons."

"Well, do the best you can!" he said.

We also collected 200 l.b.s. of great Colombian coffee!

One rainy Sunday night, Judy and I were aboard the boat at the dock when we heard the outside pay phone ring. It usually never rang, and when it did it was never for us. It kept ringing for about fifteen minutes, so I finally put on a coat and went to answer it—figuring it would stop as soon as I got near it—but it didn't. It was a friend of ours from Belmont, North Carolina.

Judy in front of *Pathfinder* before we had to leave it behind.

They were a couple we'd stayed in touch with, and were one of the few who knew our whereabouts.

My friend said that the Feds knew we were on a boat, but had no name or accurate location. Just that it was a big green shrimp boat somewhere in the Charleston area.

That, of course, was way too close for comfort. Since *Pathfinder* could only travel at twelve m.p.h. tops, we couldn't outrun the cops. That meant we had to ditch the boat! *Shit!*

The next morning, we left with only a pickup full of our personal stuff. We didn't even bother to turn the lights off in the boat. We had a little less than $1,000 in cash but didn't dare wait for the banks to open on Monday.

We went to a friend's house, told him our problem, and asked if he wanted to buy *Pathfinder*. He did, but could only come up with $3,600—the buy of a lifetime!

The cops showed up in force on a Wednesday morning with a helicopter, boats and the whole works. But they didn't find us. Our friend denied we'd sold him the boat, and there was nothing they could do about it—so they left disappointed.

That was sometime in early 1989. In September, Hurricane Hugo hit Charleston and wiped the marina off the face of the earth. *Pathfinder* was found two miles inland, looking like a broken egg lying in the tide flats.

We drove to Atlanta. It seemed to be the place we ran when we got into trouble. We dumped the truck at the airport long-term parking lot, and holed up in a motel. It was time for new names, new vehicles, new looks—the works. We made a decision to stay away from the water, since that was the second time the FBI had found us while we were living on a boat. Crying in our beer, we figured we'd lost about $300 thousand and three years of very hard work. But we couldn't look back. We had to figure out how to live on the run again.

I went shopping with some of my cashier's checks since they would buy anything, but it was hard to buy cash! In one spell, I must have bought more Rolex watches in two weeks than anyone in history. A man's gold Rolex was worth $5-6 thousand to a pawn shop anytime with no questions, and it was way safer than robbing a bank.

We left Atlanta and drove to Texarkana. There we bought a '76 canary yellow Cadillac Seville for $5 thousand in cash. Then Judy and I headed for Hot Springs, Arkansas. We rented a neat condo overlooking the lake and stayed there for two months.

We took off again and wound up in Chattanooga at the Chattanooga Choo-Choo Hilton—we stayed in an actual railroad car as a room. I worked a deal on a local watch dealer for his-and-hers Rolexes that I knew I could sell for good money later.

One day, after shopping in the local mall, we came out to discover marked and unmarked cops just crawling all over the place. Judy pointed them out to me.

"What the fuck?" I said. "They don't know we're in town—we just blew in. They aren't looking for us."

Judy continued, "Let's just get in the car and go!"

So we got out on the road, but at the first stop sign, all the cops surrounded the car. I was pretty nervous because all I had on me was the most fake-looking I.D. I'd ever made. There were police all around us with their guns drawn—they seemed to really mean business! I glanced over at Judy, and she looked like she was shitting in her pants. I knew I had to do something.

"I'm going to get out. Just stay where you are," I told her. Slowly I got out of the car and went to the guy who looked like he was in charge. "What's going on, officer?"

"May I see your I.D., sir?" the cop asked.

I handed him the chopped driver's license. "Man," I said, "I don't know why you stopped me, but I'm glad you did because

I don't know where I'm going. I'm staying at the Chattanooga Choo-Choo and I'm lost and don't know how to get back."

I noticed two cops slowly walking up Judy's side of the car, guns drawn. They got to the window, looked in, then backed away. Right at that moment, I figured we were going to be OK.

The cop handed my I.D. back, paused and said, "Go back down this road to the light and turn right and go down about two miles and you'll hit the Hilton."

As the cop turned to leave, I said, "Hey wait a minute! You can't just stop me, pull your guns out and not tell me why!"

The cops said, "We're looking for an escaped fugitive."

I said, "Oh, I hope you catch him."

Shakily, I got back in the car.

"What were they looking for?" Judy asked.

"An escaped fugitive."

"Well, guess who is one?" said Judy.

I said, "I don't know what the fuck we're going to do. We can't go back to the hotel—I just told them where we're staying."

On the news that evening, we learned they were looking for a guy from North Carolina driving a yellow Ford Granada who'd escaped and was with his blonde girlfriend. They'd run over a little local boy and killed him. It was just our bad luck we were driving a yellow Caddie! During the news report, they had some footage of the sheriff sitting at his desk talking on the phone— and there was my wanted poster on the wall next to him! Sometimes the coincidences were both scary *and* funny.

After that incident, we decided to get rid of the yellow Cadillac and get something that might pass unnoticed. We bought a 1965 Chrysler, and drove it to Alabama where we had it painted. The owner of the shop told me that I should put the car on a trailer and take it to California, because we could probably make some money on it. So we traded one of the Rolex watches for a Suburban that was in town, hitched it to a car trailer the shop owner gave us, put the Chrysler on the trailer and took off for California. But somewhere down the road and not too far outside Alabama, we got caught up in a tornado and got blown off the damn road.

We returned to Alabama, and I managed to rob a bank in Tuscaloosa. With that money, we decided to look for property in the country. On a recommendation we went up into the Tennessee hills to Vonore on the border just south of Knoxville. After staying in a trailer in the country for a while, we bought some property on top of a hill that our landlords owned. There was a foundation left on the property from a house that had burnt down, but it still had septic, water, power and a telephone that was perfect for a trailer. We bought the biggest trailer the Suburban would pull, and the company wired up the truck.

With the trailer, we went through Vonore and headed up the steep gravel road hills—when the Suburban decided not to participate. We were just a few miles from the lot when it quit; the truck lost a valve in a very tight corner in the road. I couldn't unhook the trailer, back up or let anyone around, so I walked back down the hill a couple miles and found a tractor out working in a field that I managed to flag down. Like most country folk, he was very willing to pull us up the mountain, but to get to the front of the truck the poor guy had to drive that tractor ten miles around. I was back in the truck waiting before he showed up. Judy didn't believe he was actually coming.

We settled up on that property with beautiful hills and streams, but the best part was that our landlords, the Rules, would bring us homemade biscuits and gravy every Sunday! The old man would come up every weekend and cut our grass, too. It was very hard work. The lawn sloped down away from the trailer and stopped at a small cliff that was about twenty feet straight above the road. After a few weeks of Mr. Rule coming up and cutting our grass, I started to feel a little embarrassed, so I decided to go buy a lawn mower to cut the grass myself. We went to a lawn mower shop and found a riding lawn mower that ran and looked pretty good for $200, so we loaded it in the back of the Suburban and took it home.

Our trailer had a nice deck facing the lawn. Judy watched from there as I made the first cut. I was having a good time going back and forth across the lawn working my way down the hill with a beer in one hand and the wheel of my lawn Cadillac in the other. *Shit, I missed a spot.* So I turned heading down hill, but the engine r.p.m.s went quite high, quite fast as the weight of the mower and me plus gravity really got it moving. That was when I realized that my riding mower didn't have any brakes! My velocity forward felt as if I was attaining Mach ½. I bailed out as the new mower headed toward the cliff. The only thing louder than the screaming engine was Judy's laughter. It dropped twenty feet into the ditch below. . . but didn't seem to be the worse for wear.

Getting stuck on that hill pulling the trailer when we came up was probably our downfall. Three months after we settled on top of that mountain, our auto body friend Bob in Tuscaloosa called us.

"Turn on Fox—you're on national television. Your ass needs to move!" he told me.

I told Judy to turn on the set. "Thanks," I said. "You'll probably get some heat from making this call."

"Don't worry about it, man. I'll take care of it. Let me know where you end up. Good luck and goodbye."

By the time I hung up, "America's Most Wanted" was on the TV. It was an update from a previous program, and showed pictures of us in our old Chrysler. Then they showed a generic Suburban with a photo of our trailer pasted to the back of the vehicle—it looked exactly like what we'd looked like on the road.

They were getting close again.

America's Most Wanted

"America's Most Wanted" had this information:
Aliases: Don Williams, Jay Carpenter, Don Bishop, Isiben Rogie, Clarke Roose
(Other aliases: Dan Shea, Mr. Nelson, Don Rose and Bill Young.) The FBI had their own list.
Scars and Tattoos: a panther tattoo on his left forearm, an eagle tattoo on his right forearm, a devil with an anchor and "LES" on it, swallows tattooed on his chest and a seahorse on his left shoulder.
Traits and Habits: May travel with common-law wife, Judy Wilson, who is wanted for aiding and abetting, always wears long-sleeved shirts, wears Foster Grant dark-rimmed glasses, knows how to fly single engine planes, likes race cars, known to travel and live in recreational vehicles, speaks some Spanish, enjoys sailing and boating, sailed extensively off the coast of Mexico, former Navy enlisted person, has worked as a construction worker, carpenter and sailor. Hair has white streak in middle like skunk. Traveling with a female Chihuahua named Pepper.

We put anything of value in trash bags including dishes, clothes, etc. I'd purchased a great Forest Ranger map when we were looking for some property, and it sure came in handy. The only way out of there was one road that made a big loop around the mountain. It only took one sheriff's car at the end where it came out on the main road to cover everything.

We decided to go cross-country. That meant we had to go down the mountain, across a stream and up to a fire road and we'd be in North Carolina. It wasn't far, but there weren't any roads. The trees were only three- to four-inches thick, with an old stump now and then. Of course, it was darker than hell. At the bottom of the hill was a seasonal creek that was about two-feet deep. We hit it so hard that we basically crossed on top of it, but the bank on the other side was another story. We had lots of momentum, and as we hit the bank, dirt flew through the windshield, the lights went out—we were standing on our rear bumper! The front end came down with a crash. I hit the gas as soon as we came down and tore up the rest of the incline crossways up to a logging road. Thank God for seatbelts! We were shaken up a bit, but OK. The truck looked like a meteor had hit it—twice. One headlight had gone out right away, the other one was jarred right out of its socket. We lost some exhaust parts and the front bumper, broke our windshield, and the fan was hitting the radiator, making some steam.

Thank God for duct tape! We had two rolls and needed almost all of it. I tied a seatbelt around the grill, then to a tree and backed up until the fan was out of the radiator. The radiator was torn up and had a small leak. Judy put our one headlight back in its socket, and we put a half a roll of tape on the windshield to keep it together so it didn't fall into the cab. Our rear bumper was totally gone.

We smoked a joint and snuggled up together in the cab and talked about the hardships of a life of crime.

Once we got on the paved road, we managed to buy two cans of Stop-Leak. We were hoping not to run into highway cops. Forget about the fugitive rap—they would surely impound the Suburban for being unfit to drive!

We limped back to Bob's Body Shop after unloading our stuff at our favorite motel. Bob took a bunch of photos and told us, "This one is going to be a 'before-and-after' advertising shot—tax deductible!"

Two weeks later and $400 in parts, counting the body shop bill, and the truck was a beautiful blue. It was amazing what those guys and Bondo could do. But we had to get rid of it. It wasn't dependable, and the tags were hot.

America's Most Wanted

About this time, I was just out of high school. One day, I left my truck unlocked and my wallet inside, and someone took my wallet. I was upset, but didn't think much of it until I got a knock on my door—and there stood the police! They came in, took me aside and read me my rights. I asked them what this was about, and they told me that there was a home robbery in Cornelius and that I had dropped my I.D. inside the house. I convinced them that I'd had my wallet stolen earlier that day and that I was innocent. They decided to believe me and left. But soon after, I got another call from the police. They'd found the contents of the rest of my wallet lying on a set of railroad tracks. I went to the police station to retrieve my belongings, and as I was standing there, I saw my Uncle Les on a wanted poster. Later, I saw his picture on an FBI wanted booklet in the magazine rack in the checkout line at the Fred Meyer's. It seemed he was on television all the time. I would imagine him running from the law, having a beer and smiling.

On January 4th, 1990, I made the Top Ten on the FBI's Most Wanted list—we actually heard about it from "America's Most Wanted." I thought it was no big deal—since it was only my picture up there—but we would find out I was totally wrong. Judy even had warrants for aiding and abetting a fugitive from justice that were built up to make a strong case. It changed our lives forever. There were photos everywhere, and people with incredible memories seemed to be pointing at us everywhere.

We made it back down to Atlanta and I cashed as many of my good old traveler's checks as I could. We sold the Suburban truck and bought a little diesel Volkswagen pickup. We had to make doubly sure we covered our tracks very well, even though we were running out of places to hide.

Every Saturday night, when "America's Most Wanted" came on TV was a monster because we'd have to get ready to run. We'd sit in the car with a little television sitting on our dash so we could drive off somewhere if they showed updates. We decided to go back to where people minded their own business and didn't talk to cops. It seemed best to go back to Judy's home country of southern Louisiana with the shrimper and oil rig people, the farther south the better.

We found a little five-unit apartment building in south Morgan City, Louisiana. I got a new Louisiana driver's license and new tags for the truck. I went back to "work" and robbed a bank. That sort of got the bankroll up to par.

Judy remembers: Les went in that bank and they gave him a dye pack. He only got away with about $1800. It was a lousy robbery. He had to wash it all in like nail polish remover or something. We had wet money hanging everywhere.

I went to the Coast Guard in New Orleans for an able-bodied seaman's card for the Merchant Marines—it's a good government I.D. with few background checks. It enabled me to work offshore without a passport. I avoided passports—not that they were hard to get—but getting the Social Security number is a problem, plus you have to pay taxes. So the seaman's card helped get around that.

I befriended the night guard next door to an oil rig supply company and got a job running a supply boat out to the oil rigs. It didn't pay well, but it was really low-key and paid cash. Four months later, "America's Most Wanted" had a full update that put us in Atlanta but probably around boats. We'd thought the Tennessee period would change our boat-people reputation or working around commercial boats would somehow be different, but we were wrong. They had new photos on the show. The new wanted poster had a cropped, computer-fixed photo from a North Carolina party. Usually when cameras came out, I'd disappear, but in this shot I'd been way in the background. The photo

somehow made its way into the FBI's hands, and now it deco-
rated my new wanted poster. We were out of there before the
show even ended.

In Oklahoma, I walked to a bank that I'd scheduled meeting
with a loan officer. I took out a bunch of blank cashier's checks
that I'd gotten from the North Carolina robbery. I explained to
the woman that the moving trucks with my car collection were
coming and I'd just found out they wouldn't take plastic or checks
before unloading our stuff. I wanted things to go smoothly when
my wife arrived in the other car with the kids. I told her we'd
picked a house for sale from the newspaper, and bought it from
a local real estate lady. The loan officer, of course, knew the lady,
but it was Saturday, so there wasn't much chance of them crossing paths with each other before I left the bank. By the time my
meeting was over, we'd become good friends, and she'd introduced me to everyone in the bank. I walked out of the door with
over $40 thousand in cash "to cover my expenses" in less than
two hours. She'd also given me applications for credit cards, a
savings account, C.D.s and a whole hand-full of paperwork. I
was honestly thinking of going back on Monday morning and
getting more. Greed! But I didn't. That poor lady is probably
working at McDonalds now.

Next stop was Dallas, Texas. That stupid show was telling
everyone we were traveling in a VW pickup. We had to get it
crushed so it wouldn't lead to anything. My driver's license was
tied to the truck's registration, so I needed a new license, too.
Later, we bought a piece-of-shit Bobcat station wagon, and just
started driving, trying to figure which way to point.

Judy remembers: We had to blast out of there because we
were hot. We were walking into our hotel, and our neighbor was
walking out going to get a paper or something and recognized
us. We just left without knowing what to do or where to go. So

I thought I would call my brother. When I finally got a hold of him, he was very worried. Apparently he was updated on how hot we were. We'd been on television again, and they knew the Volkswagen truck we were driving, they knew about our dog, Pepper—they knew every fucking thing.

Shortly after we got it, I ended up trading the Bobcat for a blue 1977 Space Cab Ford truck that I saw in an empty lot next to a car dealership. After buying some tires, we headed toward Mexico. We wanted to run somewhere people couldn't see that "America's Most Wanted" show! On the way, we stopped in Tucson, where we found a neat old camper for the truck that came in handy. We bought a little twelve-volt television and watched the shows before we'd check into a motel.

The truck's motor was in bad shape and needed rebuilding, so we put it in the shop. But they couldn't finish it until after Christmas. I decided to take it back before they were done. The Motel 6 we were staying in was gouging us on the daily rent and we just didn't know how long we could stay in one place. I found a fellow who, for a few bucks, helped me trade-out the motor in his driveway. What a way to spend the Christmas holiday! But we had each other and always found ways to be happy, somehow.

After we got the truck together, we blasted out of there and made for the Mexican border—back on the road again.

Surrender

Wtallied up our resources, and after we had to put new springs under the truck because of the weight of the camper, we figured we had about $800-900 bucks to live on. Judy came up with a plan to buy a box of envelopes and put $20 dollars into each one: that was our budget per day that included food, beer (major item), gas and everything else. If we wanted to go a long distance, then we'd have to save a couple of day's worth of budget money before we went. We really enjoyed the challenge.

We ended up in San Blas, Mexico. Judy worked at a gringo hamburger stand in a little tourist hotel owned by a German fellow. The way the Mexicans butchered their beef didn't result in fatty meat, so you couldn't get a good hamburger in Mexico. In San Blas, there were a lot of old hippies and gringos who we knew would love an American hamburger with cheese and fries, and Judy did a great job.

During this period, Judy learned to speak Spanish fluently. I never did, but once she learned how to conjugate the verbs it clicked for her and off she went. She's still fluent today.

Our plans kept getting interrupted by the cars we had breaking down, having our visas expire and just flat running out of money. For the next year, we went back and forth between the States and San Blas often. Sometimes we'd go back to Mexico with a load of electrical appliances. Down in central Mexico people would buy anything with an electrical cord on it since they were just getting power in most of the homes.

Judy recalls: We discovered that a Federale by the name of Ybarra in Nayarit, Mexico was on our tail. I don't know how he figured out we were hot, but somehow he knew. We asked our friend Santos to find out what was happening. He found out that the FBI had been telling people in town that we'd murdered these two old people for a car. It was a complete lie! By creating panic in the town, they hoped to put pressure on the authorities to find us quickly. So not only was our paperwork expired, but we had to go back to the States because we were hot in Mexico— and they meant business.

Sometime later, a lady in a mall started chasing me and yelling my real name: "Les, Les is that you?" I turned around and yelled at her in Spanish to stop bothering me. She said "It's me, so and so, from Roosevelt High. Don't you remember?" So hiding a hundred percent of the time was damn near impossible even out of the country.

One time, as we traveled back from Mexico, about half the way up this mountain pass outside of Sinola, we blew a rod in the truck motor, and had to pull over into the desert. While we were waiting for someone to come along, a Federale showed up.

He said, "You can't stay here!"

I told him, "There's nothing we can do. We blew a rod in the motor. I don't have money to have it towed, but if I had a lift into town I could get the parts and fix it myself. "

The Federale said, "I can't leave you here. It's very dangerous. I will call a tow truck and find one who will come for what you can pay."

So he and I sat there in the fucking desert drinking beers and shooting the cop's gun at rabbits and shit for two hours until the tow truck came. They towed us to an R.V. park, and I swear the cop came by every day to check on us. We were buddies.

Judy remembers: "On one trip, we met and befriended Peter Gilman, the author of *Diamond Head*, a book that was later turned into a movie starring Charlton Heston. We knew him as Pedro."

While we were down in San Blas, we met Don Plabio and his family who lived up the hill in a small little pueblo. Don Plabio was kind of the decision-maker when there were conflicts and such, since there were no police there. For his services in handling people's problems and small medical emergencies, the governor of Nayarit would let Plabio have cockfights at his home on Sundays, and somehow we got invited to those. All the women would be in the kitchen cooking the losers, tough old birds that had to stew a while, while the men would be out back watching the fights and drinking. One Sunday, some fellow from Guadalajara came with a truck full of fighting birds—he was obviously a pro. Plabio didn't like the guy, since he was a bit of a rogue, but he let him stay.

At the time, Don Plabio had this half-breed wolf and malamute male puppy left from their last litter. The little guy was beautiful and mostly all white with grey. That day, the puppy was running loose trying to catch the chickens.

The fellow from Guadalajara eyed the puppy and asked how much for it? Since he didn't want to sell it in the first place, Don Plabio gave him the price of one million pesos—about $330—a high price in those days. But the guy had made a bunch of money with his birds that day and said he would buy the pup. Plabio, having made a deal he didn't want to honor, spent the rest of the

183

day ducking around avoiding the guy. Suddenly, he got the great idea to dump the pup in my lap as a gift!

His problem was solved—mine was just beginning. All we needed in our little trailer was a long-haired half-wolf! But of course, we took the dog, who we discovered was named Truly, after some race horse. We needed a dog in our life since we had to get rid of Pepper. The poor little dog needed medications and vet appointments, and the Feds knew this and were looking at vet hospitals for us. Truly turned out to be a jewel. Truly was so smart, but he wanted to fight any male dog around and fuck all of the females! So we really had to watch him close. The other problem was that the wolf didn't like men—period. Women were fine, but he didn't like any man but me. He was so beautiful, you forgot his bad side fast.

We got a Bronco, but its transmission went out in Monterrey, so we sold it to our pot connection. It was time to head back to the States, but we couldn't take the dog. So we found a nice vet who would take him in. We promised to be back in thirty days. Then we took a bus headed for Texas.

As we prepared to cross the border, the first Gulf War started. The border became perilous to cross and was worrisome with rumors of all kinds swirling around. We parked ourselves in a hotel near Laredo, but still in Mexico, that had a television with CNN so we could catch up on what was going on. After a couple of days, we got a cabdriver with a passport to drive us across without any problems.

We stayed in San Antonio for a while, buying and selling cars, but weren't happy with anything and decided to move on. We ended up in Joplin, Missouri, where we found a nice Lincoln Mark IV for $500. I robbed the Webb City bank near Joplin on March 28th, 1991, and netted about $45 thousand. After some experience living in Mexico, we knew it would last a long time.

Surrender

I robbed two more banks in the Oklahoma area using the flim-flam plan with the cashiers' checks. We also bought a nice class "C" motor home from an older couple who never went anywhere but to the lake. It had been idle for several years and needed tires and such. So $10 thousand for the motor home and we were on our way. We stayed at a KOA camp and found a VW Bug, a tow bar and a new set of tires. We also found a few problems with the Bug's springs and a couple of bee's nests, but we finally pulled back into Monterrey after 112 days.

I don't remember the vet's price per day to keep Truly, but the bill came to $350. I told Judy, "If the mutt doesn't recognize us on sight he should stay here." But as the girl took us around the corner where Truly was tied up, he saw us and went berserk! For the next six years he was part of the family, and we were never apart.

Judy recalls: Everywhere we went, we were hot. We really had to be careful. I told Les, "You have got to quit robbing banks. I can't live this way much longer! You have to stop." We eventually ran out of money again, and he said he didn't know what to do. He hadn't had a paying job in a really long time, and by robbing banks he could make way more money than he could at a legitimate job. Our lifestyle cost a lot of money. I told him, "I don't know what to do either, but you better fix it." So he did. Les later turned into Mr. Fix-It.

We had many driving adventures in Mexico pulling a red Bug behind the 37' motor home. Since Mexico had a limited amount of traffic cops in these small villages they built speed bumps—but of course, the sign had no translation. We hit one at about 65 m.p.h. on an unusually good highway to Monterrey. I thought to turn the front end of the motor home, and as I hit the brakes to slow down, the VW went right by us, down the outside lane and softly landed in the left ditch.

We got it all back together in front of a big crowd watching. We laughed that it was indeed time to get out the Spanish dictionary so I could read the signs!

We decided we would visit all of the Mayan ruins. There are many ruins that set our direction and took us to Victoria and Veracruz where the giant carved heads are. From there, we got off the beaten track and ended up in Isla Del Carmen in an R.V. park owned by a gringo, but it was hardly ever used by anyone. We stayed in Del Carman for a couple months before rolling on. Next stop was Merida and the sight of Chichen Itza—which we immediately started calling Chicken Itza! The ruins were too touristy, so we went on to Cancún. There was nowhere to camp, so we continued down the coast to the Tulum Ruins. We ended up parking in the center of a beach bungalow hotel next to a generator which was my job to keep running to pay for our keep.

We'd been on the road in Mexico six months and needed to take care of the car papers that were due. Our visas were due, but nobody ever asked us for them, ever. But they did for the cars. Most of the time, if we handed a few bucks to the Customs guy we were good to go, but suddenly that didn't work anymore. The officials told us the heat was on from Mexico City, and they had to be careful. So we drove to Chetumal and then to Belize for a day, then came back and got new papers.

The word on the street was that a total eclipse was going to happen and the place to be was the Mayan ruins at Palenque—a natural park called Misol-Ha. There was a funky campground there with hook-ups for the motor home, and the entire show turned out to be great. I think every kook in the world was there recharging their crystals or themselves. It was a huge party, and there were loads of mushrooms in the fields around the campgrounds—so everyone had a grand time.

I have to admit that even though Judy and I don't believe in hocus pocus, many strange things happened during that week that led up to the eclipse. The eclipse itself was really spectacular. A pair of eagles flew over, and one person said there were no eagles around there. A wedding took place that was videotaped, but some people didn't show up on the film. Truly went nuts and howled all night. Then all of a sudden, it was over.

We took off down the highway to San Cristobal de las Cases—a real old traditional town with cobblestone streets and lots of churches and colorful Indians. There were almost no Americans, and we loved it. We found a German restaurant that had a couple of R.V. hook-ups, and we planted ourselves there. Some years previously, the owner of the restaurant was going to make a small R.V. park, but nobody ever showed up. There were two or three level spots with water, sewer and electrical hook-ups. It was the first time in a long while that we had full service just like in the U.S.

We decided if we could sell the motor home we would build a small house, so I spent a few months overhauling the Bug, with all the cheap Mexican VW parts available everywhere. Meanwhile, we started to build the house. The guy sold us a lot for $5 thousand, and there was cheap help and cement blocks everywhere. We also started making amber jewelry, from stones we found in the mine nearby, for the tourist trade.

As the little house rose from the ground, so did the fun. It seemed like every time we went to town, we would come back to find a window or a door installed—but not where the plans called for one. I spoke little Spanish, so communication with the workers had to go through the German or Judy. But no matter what he would tell them, we'd find things like a window that framed a great view—no matter that that spot was where the refrigerator was going to go!

One day, right before the house was complete, we saw a bunch of men running up past the restaurant carrying machetes—lots of them. Up the road was a small town of very religious

Indians, and these Indians had rivals. They all drank excessively, and church was an action type of event. But this seemed very different and was very scary. As the men streamed up the road, they never even looked our way. The Zapatista National Liberation Army had been fighting for the Indians' rights with the military for years. It appeared that the military was coming to end the disturbance once and for all, and the Indians were getting ready. It really wasn't a problem for the gringos except the military didn't want any witnesses, and that was the real concern. The German told us we should leave for our own safety.

The German gave us back all the money we'd spent on the house. He told us to watch the news and come back when it was over. Our car papers were due again anyway, so we headed out going south. As we left, the military was coming in convoys from seemingly every direction. We passed them with our eyes locked straight ahead. They once signaled us to pull over. I hit a left turn signal like I was pulling over, but just kept going.

In Comitan de Dominguez, we couldn't get our papers fixed because the heat was on from the Federal District of Mexico City due to political motives, so we headed further south to Parque National Lagunas de Montebello. It had seven lakes that were all a different color and very beautiful and peaceful. There were very few people at all.

After a very long and stressful day driving on the Pan American highway, we finally made it to the "point of entry" into Guatemala. Entry was a breeze as we got our tires sprayed and inspected. Truly helped a lot by going berserk at anyone who gave too much interest in our rolling combo. Our original intention was to stay a day and return to Mexico, but as we went looking for a safe place to park, we ventured deeper and deeper into the country with things getting much nicer. There were little kids in clean clothes living in mud huts waving with big smiles as we rolled by. Everywhere we stopped, people stared at the motor home. We guessed that not many motor homes ever got that far south. Some adults wanted to look inside, so we gave twenty-five-cent tours. People were completely stunned that there was an entire house inside, with a bathroom and a kitchen! A bed and a television—holy shit!

Sometimes they would bring us food; perhaps they were thinking we weren't eating since we didn't build any fires. Everyone's attitude was very positive and nice, and the sometimes-language barrier was never a problem as the locals were always happy to correct us.

We were having a great time, and everyone kept pointing us down the road to the other towns. At Guatemala's second largest city, Quetzaltenango—more commonly called Xela, which was pronounced Shayla—we found a great old central park with lots of color supplied by the local Indians. Xela was a large city, but it wasn't taken over by Burger King or McDonalds back then. We studied the R.V. campground listing, and it showed a place outside of town at a motor hotel. We found it, but there was no campground. The owner did fix us up with electricity and some water, so we stayed for a few days roaming around in the Bug.

A few days later, we were again all hooked up and on that crowded, skinny highway they call the Pan-Am; we could never figure out why it was up in the mountains instead of being down along the coast as the real main highway was. The road was so busy that the potholes couldn't be fixed properly, but it was better than anything we found in Mexico!

It was a full day's drive from Xela through most of Guatemala's thirteen volcanoes; some were active. Our little vague campground atlas told us the only other campground for R.V.s was outside Guatemala City—or as the locals called it, Guate—so we rolled cautiously into the big city. It was huge, and crammed with little cars, Bug buses and lots of trucks—a fearful driver's nightmare. To those who dare, it was just slow and hot. The only drawback was the driver didn't get much time to gawk.

Hours later, we found the so-called campground. It was a water park with five pools of varying depth and temperature, a soccer field, a restaurant and about five hookups for R.V.s. It was a welcome sight. The park closed at 6 p.m., locking us in with the entire place to ourselves most of the time. It was really great. The awning went out, and so did the chairs and table. Our site was at the edge of the action and out of most everyone's way—except sometimes on the weekends a soccer ball would go under the motor home and Truly would challenge anyone to get it!

With home established, we went on daily tours everywhere in the VW and all through the big city. We discovered the beautiful old cobblestone city of Antigua, surrounded by four volcanoes—two of which were still active. It was the old capital of Guatemala until a severe earthquake forced the citizens to move to Guate. The city was rebuilt using only buildings conforming to the original style. Hardly anyone lived there—just 10,000 people, of which about 3000 were gringos. It was the Spanish language school capital of Central America and people from all over the world came to learn. Some lived with the local families in Total Emersion Spanish Classes. We were immediately enchanted with the place.

While we were there, we enjoyed the best restaurant in town owned by some Peace Corps hippies who never went home. The owner told us he was building some condo-type apartments across from where they lived. He told us for a year's lease he would pour us a slab to park the R.V. on and give us hook-ups for our water, lights and a gate to the street for security. What could we say but, yes!

We stayed there for one year, all the while looking for someone to buy the motor home, since we had papers to renew every six months. The papers were a real hassle to acquire, since the Mexican border was 200 miles north.

During our stay there, we met many nice people. I soon developed a reputation for fixing things and being called Mr. Fix-It. I had to do something, and I really like fixing things for people and myself. I enjoyed making them happy and making their life just a little easier. I charged $10 per hour—which was excellent money down there

One day, a guy came by to look at our motor home. He was from Rhode Island or Boston or somewhere in that area, and had just married for the second time. He was on this trip with his new wife and a total of five kids of all ages. They were traveling in a mini-van, and it was just too small for the whole family. The damn kids were driving him nuts, and if he didn't find more room to separate from his gang he was nervous it would end his marriage. So we welded up a hitch so he could tow the mini-van behind the motor home, and he headed up the hill out of Antigua.

Without a camper we needed a house. We ended up finding a great house about 1600 feet above Antigua in the Western Breezes. The place was in a housing development that had sort of petered out. It was a two bedroom hurricane-type American-style cement house with a nice yard and a half-fence, half-wall with a gate, good water, a maid and her husband—when he wasn't working—and their kids were there, if we wanted. The total price was $300 month!

The view was something to kill for. We were on the side of a dormant volcano, and another was in the distance that smoked and blew hot red ashes all night with another one across the valley all with the entire town at our feet. We found home!

Our Peace Corps friends, who fixed us up the spot for the R.V., also had a couple "mini-wienies" that were little bitty, lovable dogs with no legs and no brains, but they were so lovable and cute we just had to have one. So we ended up with a boy named Choco Bananno. Then the following year, we got him a sister named Choco Mania, or Chocolate Peanut. We then had Truly and these two little guys, but our house was half-fenced and half-walled, so along with our cat we had a big family with only a few dull moments.

Truly decided to bend his rule against all males but me and adopted our gardener, Manuel. The gardener had a strong heart, and put up with the wolf's intimidation until Truly decided he was OK.

My Mr. Fix-It business was very diverse, and I was always busy. I was either fixing a washing machine or hooking up an appliance that no Guatemalan would know anything about, like a dishwasher, etc. One of my main employers was a fairly well-to-do American who ran a tourist jewelry/factory souvenir-style business that did very well. He had a large home with lots of employees who were always baffled by a washing machine or toaster or the light switches that didn't work, but one thing that happened that endeared me to him was when I figured out his water system.

The water system in Guatemala, and most other Third World countries we'd seen, always left much to be desired. Typically, if you had water to your home there was no pressure during the day because everyone simply turned on their water and let it run to fill up their *pela*—the only sink at a poor-person's home, normally just outside, which was the baby-bathing-dish-washing-clothes-washing spot. Nobody had any pressure during the day, and it only improved slightly at night. To curb this, homes had underground tanks with simple float valves that allowed any water pressure that happened to be in the line to fill them. Then another pump maintained the home pressure throughout the house during the day.

My employer had a large water tank, perhaps 8,000 gallons, but it was always running out of water, even though you could see water coming in at night. This fellow had this problem for seven years, and no one had figured it out. His Guatemalan people couldn't understand the system, and he didn't have any diagrams on how it was built. So after I dug up half the guy's water pipes, we found the problem. At night, his house pump was pumping water into the street system through a stuck check valve. After that fix he had all the water he needed—I was the hero. That one job led to many other jobs that helped me afford an old, but nice, Mercedes Benz sedan that I drove around with all my tools in the trunk. The Mercedes impressed everyone, even though it was twenty years old.

One day, I was eating at Hector's Mexican restaurant, and the owner asked for my help in starting his powerful friend's airplane. Money is power but not necessarily wisdom! Hector wanted to impress his friends with his "I'll take care of it" position. His friend had flown in the day before, and the plane wouldn't start for the return flight home. I felt it was strange that these guys could fly, but they didn't know shit about the airplane they were flying. I drove out to the landing strip used by dopers and the military, and there sitting by itself was a brand new King Air—a million-dollar plane.

They spoke no English and my Spanish was limited, so I didn't find out much except they weren't your normal dope smugglers—smugglers would have known how to fix their own troubles. I didn't know shit about that plane—I'd never been close to one, let alone sat in one! I didn't even know where the engine compartments were! I pretended to know what I was doing. I didn't pretend to be an airplane mechanic, but I didn't want to appear stupid either.

I was sitting in the left seat, after I figured out how to unlock the cabin door—one thing at a time here—and there were a maze of gauges and screens that were all blank or dead. As I turned on the engine switch, I realized there was no power. *Well, shit.* So why was there no juice? Then I noticed that the interior light switch was on but the lights weren't. They must have left the lights on all night. *OK, where then were the batteries?* I found the batteries in a compartment on the side, so I pulled up the Benz alongside and got out the jumper cables. As I was doing this, I noticed that the owners were gone. They must have gotten out of the hot sun. I felt that was for the best anyway, since if I screwed up, nobody would have known. With the jumper cables hooked up, I jumped back in the plane, and we had power. Hopping out, I adjusted the throttle on the Benz to a higher speed and looked around for some shade, too. None to be found, so I thought, what the hell, I have a good battery. Let's see if this thing will turn over.

First starboard engine on, prime and hit the start button. After about five revolutions, it started right up. It was running perfectly, and then I turned on the next port engine. The amp meters were showing a charge, so I jumped out and unhooked the cables from the Benz so I didn't fry anything and went back to the pilot's seat. I had to find the parking brakes to make sure that thing wasn't going anywhere, and they were on. Didn't even think about that before I turned on the engine—that could've been fun. Cranked the port engine and—Pop!—it started running. Both engines were sitting there idling like I really knew what I was doing! I shut and locked the battery compartment. I noticed the pilots waving and smiling as they came out from somewhere. One of them slipped me a U.S. $100 bill with many, many thanks, and they climbed in and took off! After that I was an airplane mechanic!

The next plane Mr. Fix-It repaired was a Bell 500 helicopter! Now I really didn't know anything about helicopters, but the pilot pleaded with me, saying the alternative was to fly a mechanic down from Houston. There was oil everywhere, so I took a look. Sure enough, an oil line had broken—a very obvious problem. A trip to the auto parts store for copper fittings and I had some

copper tubing, and the pilot left me alone with his bird. I re-
placed the section of line that broke, and with some solvent that
I had in the car, I cleaned most of the mess up. When the pilot
returned it looked good and didn't have any leaks. Mr. Fix-It was
now a helicopter mechanic! Ha!

Meanwhile, Judy and her girlfriend opened up a small bou-
tique full of fancy dresses, and she was also keeping the account-
ing books for the Antigua gringo paper that kept all the gringos
informed. I had a side job building clay, free-standing fireplaces,
called *chiminea*, out of big four-foot-tall vases. By cutting a hole
in the side of these big vases and placing a burner inside, they
made great fireplaces. I wasn't doing badly either—I was constantly selling out. We bought all we could find at the giant market in Guate City. In our efforts to find more and prettier vases,
we took remarkable journeys and saw most of Guatemala—it's
an amazing country.

For being in the so-called drug crossroads of Central America
we saw no hard drugs— no coke or heroin, only lots of pot, valium
and beer. It seemed lots of drugs went through Guatemala, but the
packages weren't opened there. Only once was there a big burning
of marijuana. The military decided to send a bunch of bales up in
smoke as some sort of publicity stunt, because it was advertised
in the paper. Loads of people showed up for the event at the little
fenced airfield. They must have torched a ton of pure pot. Everyone was crowded around the fence—downwind of course! And
they moved as the wind shifted—funnier than shit!

We had a friend who went to Houston for Christmas, and
when she returned, let us know that she saw my picture on
"America's Most Wanted." I was a bit worried, but nothing ever
came of it. The years started to pass by without any problems.

In December of 1995, the Biskovich family, who Judy worked
for, bought their fourteen-year-old son a computer for Christmas. I ran the power cords and telephone line to his room, but

advised his folks to use it sparingly. The telephone system was so bad that people were paying $5,000 for cell phones and systems that only sometimes worked. I never gave any thought to the boy going on the Internet. I simply thought he would be playing computer games. What could possibly happen?

In April of 1996, the FBI started a home page for their Top Ten Most Wanted and others they wanted to capture along with the U.S. Marshall's Fugitive Task Force. One day, the Biskovich kid was surfing the Net and checked out the FBI's home page— and there was a photo of Uncle Bill (as he called me)!

So that night, after we found this out, we loaded up with what we could and hit the highway headed for the Caribbean side of the country. We ended up in Puerto Barrios where there were few tourists and nobody knew who we were. I had a different set of Guatemalan I.D. that I'd never used, so our new names were Williams. We found an apartment over a tacky little marina and settled in.

Meanwhile, the kid was showing all his friends this great website, and then discovered that Uncle Bill and Anna were long gone. That's when he clicked on the "click here for more criminal history" button on the website. That apparently triggered a flag at the FBI office. When you're on the Top Ten, it never stops; there will always be a team of people who are working full-time chasing down any lead. So the kid got a call from the FBI. He told them all he knew.

That was the start of the end.

I heard a friend yelling my name at about 9 p.m. one night, and then he threw the little Guate City gringo newspaper over my fence and sped away. There was a story about me with a photo the FBI had given them on the front page. It also mentioned that our pictures were posted at every checkpoint on the highways. Our world had been violated.

We couldn't go to the bank, and we only had about $100 on us. We were driving a Subaru station wagon, and I dashed down the fishing dock to see if we could trade the car for a fishing boat. Honduras was only seventy-eight miles away, and I was sure we could get there before the cops found us. But when I returned home, I found Judy in a fit. Running had finally ground her down. She didn't know if her parents were still alive or not, and she didn't have any contact with her son. We couldn't have any contact whatsoever with any family without dire side-effects.

Judy remembers: I was done, but Les wasn't going to give himself up. He wanted to go to Honduras. We said our goodbyes to our neighbors, and went to see our good friends Dave and Diana—American attorneys living in Antigua who we'd become very close with. They told me they'd take care of me until I got arrested, because I didn't want to get nabbed by the Guatemalan police.

I decided it was time to put an end to it and made a call from a public phone to my brother, a bail bondsman. I asked him to help me work with a State-side attorney to make the legal arrangements with the embassy.

He said, "You know you're going to go to jail."

I said, "Whatever I have to do, I have to do."

There was a long pause before he said, "OK."

Just then someone came up behind me. I just knew it was the Guatemalan police. I turned around and it was Les!

He took the phone and said, "They can't have her, but they can have me."

That's how he decided to surrender and not keep on running. He gave himself up for me. He gave me his life.

I told her "The hell with it. I'll turn myself in after we discuss any deals we can make." So we packed up and made arrangements for the dogs to stay with Dave and Diana. Our friends also helped us get our surrender affidavits together. We boarded a first class bus to the capital, found a nice hotel with international phone service and I called the lawyer in Dallas. After three or four days, we made a deal to drop all the charges against Judy for aiding, abetting and harboring—which were bullshit charges anyway—so they could issue a warrant. The deal was that they couldn't attach any assets, and were to give the reward money to Judy—which was $25 thousand. The FBI were to send a plane to get me—no Guatemalan jail time.

Janet Reno oversaw the entire deal, and it was all done very professionally. I was very surprised, although they wouldn't come get us at the hotel. If we made it to the embassy, we could surrender, but if we were caught by the Guatemalans before we got there, we'd be in their custody. On Sunday, May 18th, 1996, Judy and I took a cab to the back of the U.S. Embassy in the capital and met Mr. Rivera. It was all very gentlemanly. He said that he didn't think we would show or make it that far, but it was a big coup for him. He told us that the plane was in the air and on its way.

Judy couldn't come with us because she didn't have any real I.D. She'd have to go back to the embassy on Monday to get a passport. That was the only downside, since she didn't have funds to stay for very long.

Judy remembers: They gave me $20 and told me to go find my own place. The only hotel I could afford was very low-brow, full of hookers and drug dealers. I had money for two nights and no food. I sat in my room and cried those first days, and then I got my grip on things. I needed to find my own way out. I didn't have a legal passport to get into the U.S. or an exit visa to get out of Guatemala. The embassy assholes weren't going to help me at all. So I decided to try to make some phone calls. I had to go to a nearby hotel that had a pay phone, and there a very nice American man overheard my problem and decided to help me out by giving me some money for food and a better place to stay. He also enabled me to get a black market passport, get to the border, cross and come back in so I had an entry stamp. This let me get an exit visa so I could get back home. That's how the FBI treated me, and Les had no idea. That guy was an angel just for me.

We talked and smoked in the non-smoking embassy and waited for word on the plane. Finally, we were told to move out. It was dark as we rode in the police chief's four-door pickup to the airport. There, everyone shook hands and acted glad to see me. It was very surreal. No handcuffs appeared. Then we took off.

On the four hour flight, I talked a lot to the Assistant U.S. Attorney who was in charge. He was extremely intelligent, and gave me a lot of insight to the Justice Department's ways. He was very surprised that I could tell we were flying over Cuba at the time. It was a real no-no without permission, but our government did what it wanted with other little countries.

I was in a real funk. Perhaps it was the realization that I was going back to prison—and even though that was no big deal— what bothered me was that it was going to be forever on paper. It wasn't my first rodeo though, and you never knew what the exact outcome was going to be from an adventure. I'd gotten away from them three times in the past, and forever on paper is never forever in real life.

We came straight into the Fort Lauderdale Airport. It was wet and raining on and off. When we stepped off the plane, right at that moment, the sky cleared up and it was simply beautiful, and the ground was covered in lights of all colors. The plane had pulled right up to a row of cars and vans. I was put in handcuffs and placed in a van, and off we went to Miami. First we went to the federal building and the U.S. Marshall's department. Outside, in the rain again, were television trucks and a bunch of reporters in raincoats standing around. It dawned on me that all the fuss was for me. Why? What was the big deal? I was just some bank robber who didn't believe in violence: no major chase scenes, no shootouts, just me. But it was a big deal to the media—Top Ten Fugitive Surrenders! I was also the first "Most Wanted" criminal to surrender due to being found on the Internet. One reporter rushed us, and I was speechless. I just put my head down and kept walking. The reporters stuck microphones in my face and asked stupid questions like, "How do you feel?" We walked through the reporters and into the building into peace and quiet, real serious. People were real nice and shook my hand. They were putting FBI wanted posters in my face with pens and asking for my autograph—what the hell was this?

I remember watching CNN and seeing my uncle—my own uncle!—handcuffed and walking from a vehicle. He had a host of well-dressed people walking beside him as he was just brought from South America to Miami. I remember these people were wearing dark clothes while my uncle was in a buttoned-down, light-colored shirt. Since I'd last seen him, his hair had grayed. His face showed no emotion, although there was a hint of sadness. But he was very calm and collected, as if this, too, was just another bump in the road.

I got real nervous and wanted a cigarette. So I told the people I would sign for a smoke. They told me there was no smoking, so I told them no signing. A little while later, I had myself a pack of Marlboros and a Bic lighter, and they had signed posters. They weren't your run-of-the-mill posters. They were on very nice paper—the kind you could frame. I don't know where they came from.

Surrender

They took me into a room for a couple hours worth of taking my photos. They took pictures of my entire body—even my elbows and knees!—especially my tattoos. After that, I was off to the MMDC, a federal holding center. I was issued a red jumpsuit and my personal items were inventoried. I had some stuff they wouldn't take, and a female FBI worker who was with our group told me to give her an address and she would mail it home for me. I had doubts that I would see my chain or rings again, but a couple of months later, Judy got them in the mail.

I was taken to the top floor "high power," and it was like a space ship that was round inside with painted stainless steel everywhere. They had to put their hand in this device at every door to go anywhere in the building. The top floor had a view to kill for overlooking the Miami Marina. Looking down from twelve floors at the parking lot, I saw there was graffiti painted on the ground in big letters saying "I love you." It was really neat.

Then I was alone in this room with nothing to read or listen to, but it was peaceful. I knew I wouldn't be there long since next was an appearance before the magistrate. I guessed that my next stop would be prison, most likely the next day. Sure as shit, that's what happened. I was denied bail, and ordered to be returned to custody of the Bureau of Prisons.

The Marshals told me I was going to Florence, Colorado, the Supermax federal prison. For some reason, I was sort of looking forward to seeing how they did everything. There was to be a television in your own cell, showers, meals taken to your cell and so forth, but the Oklahoma City transfer point was first, and there I was no longer a high-profile prisoner. That's when I learned I was going to a brand new United States Penitentiary that had just opened in Beaumont, Texas—and that's where I am today.

On "America's Most Wanted," I was capture number 423. I wrote AMW a letter and told them not to run that video any-

201

more, since Judy was on the outside and doing well. I told them if anyone shot her because they saw her on TV from a re-run that I would sue them. As far as I know that video is locked away.

"America's Most Wanted" turned us down for using or buying the videos or pictures that they had used to search for Les and Judy for use with this book. They denied several requests—probably due to Les's request.

Epilog

Les

My trial was bullshit. Of course I was guilty, but they didn't play fair. The crime was twelve years old, and only one person could make a statement as to what happened. There were no pictures, no fingerprints, and I was made to look different. It took them ten days to find the getaway car with no prints, etc. By the time they had the trial twelve years later, the bank didn't exist anymore. All four people who worked in the bank then recognized me and said I was dressed like such-and-such, and I left in a 1981 T-Bird—and that was all totally wrong. The FBI had told them all what happened and what to say, and they just repeated it in court. Like I said, I did it, but they didn't see it! That's the third time they've done this.

In the second trial, the fucking manager of the bank pointed out my lawyer as the robber! And on the first one, the manager said it was a Latino man 5'-7" with black curly hair that was clean-shaven and had brown eyes. She said she saw me in her dreams for months, but I had a full beard and a new driver's license with a new picture taken two days before the robbery. I had a dozen witnesses at the marina the day after the robbery who said I had a full beard. That manager bitch took advantage of me by putting out $2,500 to hire someone to steal my boat

United States Penitentiary Medium Security, Beaumont, Texas. 2007.

from the Bahamas and bring it back to Miami so the Feds could seize it. All because she wanted it for herself!

The stories continue, but yeah, the trial was bad! It may sound like I'm bitter, but really, I knew what would happen if they caught up with me.

It still baffles me why they got so upset. No one was ever hurt or harmed, and I landed on the Top Ten—the first time they put someone on it with no violence. So now I'm sixty-nine and have fifty-three years left on my sixty-five-year sentence.

Oh well, I did have a great life, have a wonderful wife and did stuff most people just dream about. Now I'm retired, have full room and board and full medical in a hundred-million dollar complex. It sure doesn't sound too bad that way!

The other day I came back from the chow hall, and my case worker was going crazy looking for me. The parole board examiner was there to see me, but no one told me I was on the docket. So I had five minutes notice to get my thoughts in order. At my age it usually takes two- to three-hours! I had a few items to bring up, and they were complicated and lengthy to explain. I wasn't in a good mood.

The examiner was a young black lady who seemed to have a grasp on things, but the meeting went badly from the moment she asked me if I had anything to say.

We started with my court orders, which she knew nothing about. Or the fact that I surrendered. Or that there are favorable letters in my file. Or that my record has been clean for at least six years, etc. She didn't know about Judy waiting or anything like that. I really blew up, and told her she had the ability to rule over my future life without knowing any of the background. She didn't come prepared at all!

All she wanted to do was talk about my escape. I told her that anyone facing forty-five years in prison would take the opportunity to pick Door Number Two and go free if given the chance. The only other option is to accept prison and dismiss any chance of freedom.

I need to figure out what is going on at the court in El Dorado since these people have no intention of releasing me. I believe that no one who makes the Top Ten Most Wanted list ever goes free. More recently, I've filed a motion to recant my guilty plea, since the government hasn't lived up to their deal in the plea agreement.

We'll see.

I remember when my sister Jeannie came to see me with my nephew Dane in 1985. The Marshals had sharpshooters on the roof of the jail when she came to visit. It sure was funny. Somehow I think they had the idea she was coming to get me! And I walked out a couple days later, but it just doesn't seem like it was twenty-five years ago. I guess for me my sister doesn't change. Dane calls her Mum. Same nice voice, same handwriting, and nobody could have a better sister than I. Oh yeah, a loving, concerned personality, too, and a great mom.

Stay tuned! Perhaps escape number four is coming soon!

Dane

Les will call me periodically when money allows or he has a question about the book or to chat. He calls Judy and Mum on a more regular basis. Calling cards cost money, as does everything in prison that is not absolutely vital and provided by the prison. There's a small store where he can buy almost anything he needs. He depends on it for everything he needs including aspirin, snacks, extra clothes, toothbrushes, etc, but he does get three hot meals a day and extremely minimal health care. Les's family members send him money that he uses for everything. Actually, they send it to him via the prison system and they put the money in his account.

Les has to stock-up on rations in his cell since every hurricane warning results in a lock-down, or whenever there is a fight, gang war or a murder in the prison—which there seem to be many of every year—they go into lock-down. In that event, Les gets a peanut butter sandwich and water once a day and that can go on for a week or more. The last hurricane, that damaged Galveston badly, put them in lock-down for a week, and the facility operators and guards mostly went home. Les rode out the hurricane in his ground floor cell by himself without being given water or food for over three days. So Judy is good about preparing Les for emergencies so he can purchase items from the store to stock up so he's not alone with his peanut butter sandwich. We also send him books and magazines from time to time, since he'll read anything you send him. Books from bookstores are easy to get to him, but you should have seen the trouble it was for me to get him review copies of this manuscript. I'm sure half the prison staff has a copy of some version!

Epilog

Les and Judy Rogge, USP Beaumont, Texas. Christmas 2000.

I find it amazing that when Les does call that he is always happy. Somehow he finds a way to see that the glass is half-full, and he hardly ever seems upset or angry, even though his conditions are very tough. I like to tease him by telling him I'm having a beer while I'm talking to him, and he gives me shit because that is one thing that he loved that he can't buy in the prison store. The only alcohol that he gets is made in a toilet.

Judy visits Les at least once a month and has for the past decade. He was transferred to Beaumont Federal Correctional Complex not just because it was new at the time or housed the high security risks, but on Judy's request. It's only a relatively short drive for Judy to the visiting room where she can sit and chat with him for a good portion of the day. They sit in a painted cinderblock room with rows of chairs that are overlooked by a high-rise security desk, overhead cameras, one-way glass, bars and razor wire for as far as you can see. And that's the medium security portion of the prison. The high security, where Les spent the first ten years of his sentence, has high towers surrounding the facility. The razor wire is strong and deep; they sure the shit don't want anyone to leave—and I don't know that anyone has yet. As I was driving in the first time I visited Les in the High, I paused to take a picture of the outside of the facility. From many hundreds of yards away a loud speaker came on telling me not to stop and take pictures. Apparently they had a rifle with a big scope watching me approach the prison in my rental car. I was a threat in my Dodge Neon.

As you sit and watch Judy and Les interact, they have playful banter that many relationships can only envy. They catch up on what's been going on and reflect back and share their grand stories of times on the run and their different points of view on the same stories. As Les argues his point of view he looks up to the ceiling lights for help in remembering how the good times actually happened. Then he puts his hand on her knee, as they sit side by side facing the security, as if to say *OK, you're right*, with a slightly embarrassed grin. It dawned on me when I saw this, that this was their relationship for the past twenty-seven years. They

Epilog

didn't apparently talk about the hard or serious times much back in the day since they have slightly different versions, but they want to get their stories straight with one another and their playful debates are extremely enjoyable. Their playful and healthy relationship is still strong after fourteen years behind bars.

Judy says, "I still get goose bumps, and he makes my heart flutter when I see him even today. I miss just sitting down and talking alone."

For closing in on his seventies, Les is very healthy. Perhaps it's due to his lack of nine-to-five jobs, or lack of stress which only a psychologist could understand, but he is one of the healthiest seventy-year-olds that I know. He participated in an over-fifty football game the other day and was actually tackled, so maybe that will tell you. His noticeable white spot in his hair has gone silent as his hair is now completely snow white and he seems to wear his white, coarse mustache proudly. Although he has lived a life of crime, he seems an honorable and loving man who would do anything for you. You simply can't judge a book by its cover—although maybe you can this one.

Les is due to be released on 2-10-2047.

About the Author

Dane Batty is a technical writer, biographer and designer. He is a proud husband and father of two and holds an MBA from George Fox University. He lives near Portland, Oregon with his family and enjoys motocross racing and golfing on the weekends.

References

William Gough, "Seattle native sought in bank robberies." *Seattle Times,* Saturday, January 22nd, 1983.

Don Fair, "A fugitive & his gang have robbed 14 banks." *Seattle Post-Intelligencer,* Saturday, January 22nd, 1983.

Mike Shepard, "Bank robber still on loose – Seattle bandit breaks out of Latah County facility." *Moscow Pullman Daily News,* Monday, September, 30, 1985.

Mike Shepard, "Latah sheriff moves to prevent escapes." *Moscow Pullman Daily News,* Tuesday, October 1st, 1985.

Christena Colclogh, "Bad connection – Man revealed as bank robber after he wires boy to Internet." *Seattle Post-Intelligencer,* Friday, June 21st, 1996.

Molly Moore, "How 'Mr. Fix-It' got caught." *Washington Post,* 1996.

"Internet posters taking byte out of crime." *Journal-Tribune,* Marysville, Ohio Saturday, November 30th, 1996.

"Americas Most Wanted" website. August, 2008. www.amw.com

LaVergne, TN USA
07 April 2011
223278LV00002B/95/P